Safe Senior Drivers

A Guide
for a Critical Time

Edited by Phil Berardelli

Mountain Lake Press
Mountain Lake Park, Maryland

Safe Senior Drivers
A Guide for a Critical Time

COPYRIGHT © 2012 PHIL BERARDELLI

ALL RIGHTS RESERVED

LIBRARY OF CONGRESS
CONTROL NUMBER:
2012945258

PUBLISHED BY
MOUNTAIN LAKE PRESS
24 D STREET
MOUNTAIN LAKE PARK, MD 21550

ISBN-978-0-9814773-9-8

PRINTED IN THE UNITED STATES OF AMERICA

DESIGN BY MICHAEL HENTGES

When I die, I want to go peacefully
like my grandfather did, in his sleep – not screaming,
like the passengers in his car.

– Jack Handey

CONTENTS

INTRODUCTION

by Phil Berardelli

I published my first book on safe-driving techniques in 1996. It was the natural outcome of an article I had written two years earlier for The Washington Post about teaching my daughters how to drive.

When I began the project, I admit, I was interested more in making a buck than in the particular subject of the book. Such is the nature of freelance writing. Ideals are fine, but you've got to pay the bills. On the other hand, in order to make that buck, I had to produce something worth buying. So I set out to expand my original article into a detailed blueprint to help parents teach their teenagers to become, as the book's eventual title stated, Safe Young Drivers.

Two things emerged from that process – along with a book that has remained in print and sold reliably for over 15 years. First, I began a detailed observation of our society's driving habits that I have continued to this day. Second, I became and remain truly appalled by what I observed. As a society we are damned incompetent, dangerously so, behind the wheel, which is why tens of thousands of us die on the roads each year, and millions are injured.

That assessment led me to my second book, The Driving Challenge: Dare to Be Safer and Happier on the Road, which I first published in 2001, I updated as an ebook in 2011, and the lessons from which I have adapted here.

Safe Senior Drivers: A Guide for a Critical Time is the third in the series, and it's quite different. For one thing, I decided early on that the subject was far too complex to cover on my own. Helping a senior driver – which I will soon become myself – is not nearly as clear-cut a task as devising an instructional program for teens. It isn't even as direct as analyzing the problem of aggressive driving and devising methods to combat our collective bad habits. No. Driving among seniors is the most difficult and complex problem of all. That's why I've called on five other authors, each of whom has amassed a particular field of expertise, to help me:

Dr. Allan F. Williams, former chief scientist for the Insurance Institute for Highway Safety, puts the senior-driving issue into perspective.

Lidia Wasowicz Pringle, my former colleague at United Press International and a specialist in health issues, focuses her formidable research and interviewing skills on the experiences of individual seniors and on organizations that have established programs to help.

Dr. Robert A. Comunale, a physician in family practice for many years, discusses how advancing age can translate into specific physical liabilities.

John Matras, a lifelong auto writer, examines how technology is helping to extend the tenure of and protect our seniors on the road.

And Jessie Thorpe, my co-editor and publishing partner, connects the many themes of the book in a personal account of how this issue can affect families.

Together, we hope to give you the best tools available to manage driving in your senior years, or to manage the transition of your parent or loved one into a less active – and eventually inactive – driving reality.

PART I
The Road to Driving Retirement

1. A Growing Problem – or Not?

by Dr. Allan F Williams

I want to prolong driving as long as I can, so I belong to a group that walks 3 miles a day and to an aqua exercise class. I'm well aware of what happens when you can't drive anymore, having a friend who had her keys taken away by her doctor when she was 84. She takes the bus whenever she can, but it gets very lonely when you can't hop into your car whenever you've got places to go and people to see.

– Gini M., 73

Next time you're at a social gathering, try bringing up the subject of senior drivers. Chances are you'll elicit a story or two about someone's aged parent who insists on staying behind the wheel despite obvious difficulties doing so.

It's become a common theme. Families across the country are involved in disagreements – sometimes wrenching and deeply divisive – over the driving competency of their senior members, with seniors typically claiming fewer problems than their children, relatives and friends have been noticing.

Get used to it. The Baby Boomers have reached retirement age. That bumper crop of postwar babies born between 1946 and 1964 has already begun to swell the portion of Americans age 65 and over – estimated by the 2010 Census to be 40 million, about 13 percent of the population. By 2030 the number of U.S. seniors is expected to reach 70 million, or 20 percent of the total. Of those, nearly 10 million will be age 85 and over – and many will still be driving. Our culture on wheels is dug in, as those of us in our golden years hang onto our car keys longer and rack up more miles than ever.

The prospect worries highway safety officials. Will this surge in senior drivers be accompanied by a spike in motor vehicle crashes and fatalities after decades of decline?

It's possible. One reason is crash demographics. The high rate among teenagers begins to decline among twentysomethings and continues to ease on a long, slow curve until about age 70, when the incidents start rebounding. Then they jump markedly after age 80.

Fears about a coming crash epidemic caused by older drivers also get stoked occasionally by sensational incidents, such as the one in July 2003 when an 86-year-old man accelerated into a crowd of pedestrians at a Santa Monica, California, farmers' market, killing 10 and injuring 63.[1]

Lawyers claimed that their client had confused his car's gas and brake pedals.

Then there was the episode in October 2006 in Orlando, Florida, when an 84-year-old woman crashed her car through the front window of a Sears department store and plowed through to a cash-register counter, hitting a concrete support pillar.[2]

Rescuers found that the woman's foot had become stuck between the gas pedal and the floor.

And in two separate but back-to-back incidents near Boston in June 2009, a 93-year-old man crashed into a Walmart entrance, injuring several shoppers, and a 73-year-old woman plowed into a group at a war memorial, injuring several more. [3, 4]

Misconceptions

All true, but do these incidents really justify widespread fear? Well, yes and no. Yes, because on an individual level the problems of a senior driver can be serious and even dangerous, given his or her physical or mental impairments. No, because seniors as a group have the lowest crash, fatality and injury rates of any age range.

Why the dichotomy? For one thing, even though seniors are driving more and longer, their licensing rates and average miles driven are lower than for younger drivers, and these trends should hold up even with the influx of the Baby Boomers. For another, though the oldest seniors post higher crash rates per miles driven than all age groups other than teens, they're also more likely than younger drivers to reside in dense urban areas, where crash rates are higher than on freeways and multilane roads.

Bottom line: If you examine the statistics carefully, you'll find that all but the oldest seniors remain among the safest drivers on the road.

The Fragility Factor

There is one area where senior drivers tend to fare worse than their younger counterparts: injuries and fatalities. The reason is physiology. Our resident geriatric specialist, Dr. Robert Comunale, will cover this topic in more detail, but basically the problem has to do with the growing fragility of the human body that can begin as early as the 60s and accounts for more than half of senior deaths on the road.[5]

In other words, many if not most of senior fatalities and injuries on the highway occur because the drivers' aging bodies are beginning to let them down. They die in situations that younger drivers tend to survive. That goes for their passengers as well, because they also tend to be seniors. And in terms of fatalities, senior drivers mostly harm themselves. The frightening instances I described above notwithstanding, seniors tend not to kill others on the road.

A Favorable Trend

Taken altogether, the crash-involvement picture for seniors is decidedly mixed. They aren't the menace they're sometimes portrayed to be. In fact, there's even some good news: Over the past decade the crash risk for senior drivers has been declining more than for middle-age drivers. Between 1997 and 2008, for example, fatal passenger vehicle crashes per senior driver fell by 37 percent, compared with a 23-percent drop among drivers ages 35-54. Moreover, drivers ages 80 and up experienced an even steeper decline: 49 percent.[6]

These trends were quite unexpected. If fatal crash rates for senior drivers had mirrored the trends for middle-age drivers during these years, about 10,000 additional seniors would have been killed. Injuries and property damage also decreased more for seniors than for the younger group, and even the likelihood of an older person surviving a crash is getting better.

Frankly, we in the highway safety community don't fully understand the reasons for these findings, but it may have something to do with improvements in the health and physical conditioning of seniors, as well as advances in emergency medical services and trauma care.

Self-Regulation

There's another possibility related to this unanticipated good news: Seniors may be doing a proper job of policing themselves, modifying their driving as they sense diminished abilities to negotiate the roads.

I suspect many do this on their own or in response, perhaps reluctantly, to the advice – or maybe pleadings – of family or friends. We know about some of this from surveys, in which seniors say they are limiting their driving, a practice that increases with age. We also know that seniors with impairments in vision, memory, physical functioning and various medical conditions are most likely to do so.

The self-limiting sometimes involves giving up driving entirely, but for those still on the roads it typically involves driving less often, avoiding nighttime hours and confining trips to shorter distances within well-known areas.

Some of it also could be because seniors are heeding the materials distributed by the American Automobile Association, AARP, and the American Medical Association, among other organizations. All are working to help seniors and their family members understand how aging affects driving. They have provided useful information on the effects of medications and health conditions, and in general how to cope with difficulties experienced on the roads.

Assistance from Passengers

Another factor could be enhancing the driving safety of seniors: passengers. It's well known that passengers can be deadly for teenage drivers, with the mutual horseplay and distractions creating a greatly elevated risk for major crashes.

For seniors, however, the presence of passengers is protective. New research suggests that crash rates are lower when seniors drive with a passenger than when they drive alone, and the protection is strongest for older male drivers.[7]

What's going on? It turns out that passengers can be helpful copilots, keeping drivers alert, assisting with navigation, warning of impending hazards, and operating the radio, heat and air-conditioning controls, or using the cell phone.

It makes sense. Many older driver/older passenger combinations are married couples who have long-established ways of interacting – outside as well as inside the vehicle. Also, among senior couples, the person who is more able tends to do the driving.

Sticky Questions

Now here's the bad news – or, more precisely, the imponderables that currently surround senior drivers. For instance, exactly how well do they compensate for impairments, either alone or using help from their passengers?

It's difficult to know. Though many seniors show no signs of impairment that would affect their driving, others do and need to make adjustments. But we lack good data on how they're sorting it out.

For one thing, seniors might not even recognize they are developing certain visual defects, such as a narrowing field of view. For another, they may sense a condition that is negatively affecting their driving but haven't tried to compensate for it. Or, they might be amenable to persuasion from their spouse or regular passenger, but that person hasn't noticed the condition yet. In both cases these are not easy adjustments for seniors to make.

Also, a senior thinking about hemming in or giving up driving might be constrained by the logistical dilemma of finding alternative transportation, something that often requires the help of family members.

What if a debilitation begins to appear and the senior has no ready alternative to driving? In some states, physicians are legally obligated to report certain medical conditions to licensing authorities. Does that mean the senior will delay or stop going to the doctor to hide that condition?

What about the physician? Many doctors are reluctant to counsel their patients about driving decisions – especially long-standing patients. Instead, they may refer the senior to an occupational therapist or a driver-rehabilitation program. Good steps, but such options can be expensive.

Then there's the male angle. Many older men insist on driving indefinitely, and studies indicate that men – no surprise – are the least likely to self-regulate. The result is a large but unknown number of seniors who are continuing to drive but should not.[8]

New Trends

All of this represents a new way of framing senior-driving issues. It's a departure from earlier times, when we would focus more on impairments and on identifying those who should be removed from the roads.

Two shifts have been under way for some time – in the United States and in other countries where seniors make up a significant portion of the driving population. One involves discarding the notion that links an elevated crash risk with all senior drivers. Instead, researchers and safety officials have begun focusing on the specific portions of the demographic at greatest risk.

The second and related development recognizes that the core of the senior crash problem primarily involves people with conditions that no longer allow them to drive safely, conditions that are irreversible, such as severe dementia or uncontrolled seizures. The question, then, becomes which older drivers are at higher risk?

Variations

Given what we've learned, it's clear that restricting driving based solely on age or common stereotypes is not appropriate policy. Senior drivers encompass a wide age range, spanning more than 20 years. Some 85-year-olds are more capable drivers than 65-year-olds, and within any age there is a broad range of competencies.

The generalizations work both ways. You can read much in the popular literature about the healthy, happy "golden age" that combines wisdom and competence. It's different from the past, when seniors were often portrayed negatively.

But glamorizing old age has its limits as well. For example, in Susan Jacoby's book *Never Say Die: The Myth and Marketing of the New Old Age*, she writes that among the "old old," meaning those in their late 80s and beyond, degenerative, chronic and irreversible conditions become increasingly common.

Bottom line: Mobility and independence for seniors are important, but maintaining these attributes eventually becomes a problem for everyone as they age. We just don't know when and for whom.

When the Government Steps In

When a senior's driving becomes unsafe, and he or she hasn't been deterred by family or friends, state licensing agencies become the backstop – with license renewal the instrument – for driver reevaluation. A license in most states is valid for 4 to 6 years. A few states allow licenses to be renewed electronically or by mail, but in most cases drivers must appear in person, pay the license fee, and have a new photograph taken, along with taking a vision test.

Furthermore, over half of the states employ different procedures for drivers older than a certain age, generally 65 or 70. These procedures can include shorter intervals between renewals, along with the in-person requirement, the required vision testing and in some cases road testing.

At renewal time, licensing officials can take the measure of an applicant's appearance to gauge whether he or she needs further assessment. Vision tests also may reveal issues, though they typically measure only visual acuity and field of vision, which do not necessarily relate well to crash risk.

Seniors can also be referred to licensing agencies by police, physicians or other medical personnel, and family and friends. A few other referrals come from crash and violation records or from the courts. In many states, medical advisory boards composed of physicians and other healthcare professionals can help determine a senior's capacity to drive.

Age-Based Failure

One area where licensing officialdom is currently ill-serving seniors involves age-based, mandatory assessment programs. The main reason is no one has developed a screening method that accurately predicts people at elevated risk for crash involvement. It raises the possibility that some people will be falsely – and unacceptably – branded as crash prone.

Even in the states where medical boards assist in decisions about license retention, accuracy remains an issue. Usually the process begins when a senior's physician is asked to complete a report about the patient's ability to continue to drive. The American Medical Association provides guidelines for judging medical fitness, but many physicians have not received sufficient training or gained enough experience to render such judgments reliably. They also may be reluctant to help pull the keys from a long-term patient. So, many just kick the question back to the DMV and recommend a driving test.[9]

Some studies have shown that vision testing of seniors is associated with lower fatalities, possibly by screening out those with serious visual deficits. But other studies have not been so promising. In Sydney, Australia, for example, which requires medical evaluations regarding fitness to drive beginning at age 80, and road tests beginning at age 85, researchers have found no discernible safety benefits compared with older drivers in Melbourne, which imposes no such requirements.

Likewise, comparisons between Finland's senior-driver requirements (medical checks for license renewal from age 70 on) and Sweden's (no age requirements) found no significant differences in crash rates.

Here in the United States, an extensive study found no safety benefits for state-mandated vision tests – something that contradicted earlier research. The study reached the same conclusions for road tests, more frequent license renewal and in-person renewal for drivers ages 65-84. [10]

The only policy that can be scientifically linked to lower fatality rates is in-person renewal for drivers ages 85 and older. Of course, this might also mean most senior drivers choose to let their licenses lapse rather than undergo mandatory reassessment. If so, it raises two worries: 1) Some could be giving up on driving prematurely, and 2) others might be driving on expired licenses, hoping no one will notice and that they can stay out of trouble.

Even when seniors do give up their licenses, it doesn't necessarily mean they're out of danger. They may become pedestrians, which can be even more dangerous for them, in terms of crash involvement.

Whatever the data show, however, public support is growing for mandatory, frequent and strict assessments of senior drivers, spurred on by crashes like the one in Santa Monica. States governments are responding. Over the years more have been adding age-based assessment policies – and no states have removed them.

Mobility Is the Key
Despite the – to use a polite term – morass of licensing policies that do not work, the field is showing promise in other areas. For example, the regulatory focus is narrowing to encompass only those seniors deemed most at risk. And new efforts are under way to maximize mobility for seniors while de-emphasizing their use of motor vehicles.

These developments aren't exactly new. Both topics were

featured in a 2001 report by the Organisation for Economic Co-operation and Development.[11]

The report proposed that senior driving safety could best be managed by targeting those indisputably at risk, leaving safer seniors with the most mobility options.

The OECD report proved to be a landmark in the highway safety community. Its authors recommended revoking licenses based on whether a senior's potentially disabling condition could be treated, the extent to which it affected driving safety and whether the individual could compensate for its effects – plus balancing risk against the costs of reducing the individual's mobility.

As a result, the Older Drivers Project, an initiative of the American Medical Association and the U.S. National Highway Traffic Safety Administration, endorses in principle revoking a senior's license only when the safety of the driver cannot be assured by any other means. The AMA and NHTSA (pronounced NIT-sah) also note that the project's primary objective is to preserve mobility. And their position incorporates the idea that medical conditions constitute a safety problem only in the absence of self-regulation or compensation.

It's a critical factor. Emphasizing mobility recognizes how important it is to keep seniors independent and socially connected. The approach also acknowledges how the loss of mobility can lead to depression, lessen the ability to obtain medical care, and reduce contact with family, friends and acquaintances.

A driver's license is a marker of successful aging; losing it can be a devastating blow, both psychologically and practically.

Enter Graduated De-Licensing

Some states have likewise accepted the idea of maximizing mobility for senior drivers. As part of that concept they are enacting what is essentially the counterpart of graduated licensing for teenagers. Just as those programs incrementally increase privileges for young drivers as they gain age and experience, the new strategy, commonly called graduated de-licensing, allows essential driving but incrementally removes seniors from situations that have grown particularly risky for them.

Graduated de-licensing laws help to transition seniors from an unrestricted license to no license. Unlike beginning drivers, however, who share inexperience and a minimum age, seniors must be judged on a case-by-case basis. Nevertheless, some common areas have emerged.

For example, one of the first restrictions is speed-related, requiring seniors to avoid heavily traveled expressways and roads with high speed limits. Another prohibits driving after dark. Eventually, a graduated de-license allows seniors to drive only in their own neighborhoods or within a certain distance of their homes.

But even at that stage, the restriction allows essential driving, such as for medical care, shopping, and contacts with friends and family.

This isn't exactly a new approach. Every state can issue restricted licenses to drivers of any age. It's just that few states have exercised this authority. Instead, licensing is usually an all-or-nothing decision – the individual in question is either allowed to continue to drive or is stripped of a license.

The mindset seems to extend to driving examiners. Anecdotal evidence suggests they likewise make all-or-nothing judgments: If a person can't drive adequately in some situations, the examiner will refuse to approve a license renewal, concluding that the individual shouldn't be allowed to drive at all.

But times are changing. Restricted licenses are on the increase and, in the case of the growing senior driving population, not a moment too soon. It's an equitable arrangement that balances public safety with allowing seniors the maximum practical freedom on the road. It's also an arrangement that seniors are likely to respect, because it removes some of the fear and reluctance they can feel about the license-renewal process.

Of course, the success of graduated de-licensing will depend on how humanely and patiently our motor-vehicle departments treat seniors during the evaluation process. The truth is that seniors dread the trip to the DMV at renewal time even more than the rest of the driving population. Along with the wait times involved, and the often impersonal nature of the process, they also worry about whether they will be allowed to continue their lives behind the wheel.

Another Possibility: Tiered Testing

Given the size of the driving population, any program that tries to screen driving fitness on an individual basis is going to be difficult. The most important challenge: making correct judgments.

That's why some states have been experimenting with a concept called tiered testing. For example, California is studying the use of a three-tiered assessment for drivers of all ages. License-renewal screenings include observing for obvious physical limitations, coupled with testing for vision, cognition and knowledge of the rules of the road. Whoever fails must take a road test.

Testing behind the wheel might seem like the gold standard for assessing driving competence, but even those results aren't always definitive. That's why Maryland has begun a program to identify practical screening measures that produce the highest degree of accuracy. The effort involves a battery of tests that seem to be able to predict future crash risk. DMV staffers administer the tests to drivers who have been referred by the police or others. They combine the results with recommendations of a medical advisory board.

Other countries also are pursuing the goal of balancing senior mobility and public safety. Australia has taken the lead in developing tiered testing that can be used in both Australia and New Zealand. The consensus so far is that no existing screening methods are sufficient by themselves to make a pass/fail call, but they can be used along with other information in judging fitness to drive. Inevitably, the process involves some educated guesswork.

Iowa's Approach

Among the 50 states, Iowa has promoted tiered screening the most extensively. There the DMV requires in-person license renewal every five years for drivers under age 70 and every two years for those 70 and older.

Vision tests are given by the state Department of Transportation, and the department encourages staffers to be proactive in identifying drivers who are potentially unfit to remain on the road and should be evaluated further. Police, family or physicians can also recommend reexamination. The process includes road tests, and drivers can choose to take the test at licensing offices or at other locations near their homes. If they choose to take the nearby test, however, they will receive some kind of geographic restriction.

If drivers pass the road test they may avoid license restrictions. They may also pass but with some limitations. Or, if they fail, the examiners will discuss their deficiencies and offer the option of taking the test two more times. Continued failure results in license suspension.

When drivers receive restricted licenses, their limitations are individually tailored and can include one or multiple restrictions, such as no driving at night or in inclement weather, staying off interstates or freeways, and driving only near their residences.

So far, the Iowa approach's effect on crash risk isn't known, but one study suggests that restricted license holders are showing a high degree of compliance, with the possible exception of geographic restrictions. The reason seems to be that seniors are already limiting their driving to some degree. Also, the prospect of restrictions seems to have reinforced decisions seniors were already considering.

Improving Vehicles and the Driving Environment
If we're going to take on the challenges of keeping senior drivers safe, we can't concentrate exclusively on their ability to negotiate the roads. After all, we're talking about a segment of the population that numbers in the tens of millions and is growing. To be comprehensive and fair we also need to improve our vehicles and the driving environment.

John Matras, our resident automotive writer, examines this

subject in more detail. But in brief, several vehicle-design changes intended to prevent crashes are beginning to enter the vehicle fleet. They include electronic stability control, which can reduce the risk of fatalities even in single-vehicle crashes, as well as lane-departure warning systems and blind-spot detection – aka side-view assist.

What we don't yet know is how well seniors will interact with these systems and whether the new technologies will improve or distract from the driving task.

Needless to say, occupant protection in crashes remains a major concern, particularly for seniors, whose bodies become increasingly frail as they age – another topic examined by Dr. Comunale. But we do know that further advances in airbags, head restraints, and other devices that limit the force of restraints during a crash can improve survival chances and reduce injuries.

Yet another consideration: features that make driving more comfortable for seniors, such as brighter and bigger displays and controls, adjustable pedals, and better seat adjusters. John Matras examines these factors and others to help seniors select the best vehicles to meet their driving needs.

In terms of environmental changes, we all know what's required: Better visibility of signs and roadway markings can help all drivers, particularly those with visual deficits. Intersections, which can befuddle seniors, can be improved through dedicated left-turn lanes, left-turn arrows and other modifications that reduce maneuvering complexity.

Yes, they're controversial, but many highway safety experts favor replacing traditional intersections with roundabouts. Granted, some senior drivers would need retraining to learn and execute the give-way rules of roundabouts. But these configurations have demonstrably eliminated some of the problems associated with crashes – such as red-light running – and they inhibit speeding.

End of the Road
Despite every effort to prolong their mobility, inevitably senior drivers will have to give up their keys and manage the rest of their lives

without this privilege. Lidia Wasowicz Pringle, our veteran health reporter, explores this topic at length beginning in the next chapter. But some aspects are clear. One is that licensing agencies recognize the need for counseling about alternative transportation opportunities, and social workers and others also may need to get involved to assist in lifestyle adjustments.

Alternative transportation may be the most critical issue facing seniors at the end of their driving tenure. Sometimes the solution is simple: Family members, relatives or friends living nearby assume transport duties. In some communities, van services with volunteer drivers pick up the slack.

In other areas, aging-in-place organizations are emerging. One of their main functions is taking senior non-drivers to medical appointments, on shopping trips, and to church or social events, while keeping tabs on their charges in general. Senior-living facilities generally provide transportation.

These are important functions. The end of a driving career can be disappointing and frustrating, but a supportive and caring community can help make up for the loss.

2. America's Car-Centered Lifestyle

by Lidia Wasowicz Pringle

When I immigrated to the United States from Poland 50 years ago, the greatest – and easiest – adjustment I had to make was to Americans' dependence on their own cars. I recall the thrill of purchasing and driving my first car, which made me feel free and independent as never before. If I had not retired to Mexico, where, as in Poland, the cultural focus is on public, not private, transit, I'd probably still be driving!

—Janina G., 89

Whether your memory is firm or fading, odds are the recollections of your first driving experience remain solidly intact.

Just ask Judy Mark, 73, of Tiburon, California. She recounts in vivid detail how, 60 years ago, her physician father took her along on a house call, asked her to scoot next to him in the front seat and permitted her to steer, while his own hand gingerly cupped the wheel in case of a sudden and necessary readjustment.

With the debut of Chrysler's automatic transmission, Mark's father even allowed her to put the car into "drive" and "reverse." By the time she turned 15, she "couldn't wait to get my first license." She aced the driving portion of the exam but agonized over the 10 written questions.

"My father stood behind me and told me the answers," confesses Mark, who is still driving – though with a much improved understanding of the rules of the road.

She had to wait four years for her first car, a 1953 Chevrolet passed down from her mother. It served her well but wasn't serviced in return. By the time she decided to replace the tires, the treads had worn so deeply she had a flat on the way to the shop. Her father once again came to the rescue, a shock to her sense of being "exhilaratingly liberated" behind the wheel.

To this day, the automobile revs up that all-American image of freedom and independence, of the ability to traverse short distances or vast expanses at one's will and leisure. No other culture has ever so assimilated this personal mode of transport as its driving force. Steer through a field of aspirations and you'll hit upon the reasons.

"(The) American psyche is based on freedom of movement," reflects John D. Locher, 51, senior-driver ombudsman at the California Department of Motor Vehicles in Sacramento.

"Many don't realize this," he explains, "but America's greatness came not from the Industrial Age but from the ability to [move] goods from one part of the country to the next. Because of trains, a farmer who made chairs in Vermont was suddenly able to reach customers in Minnesota. This freedom of travel was the beginning of our love affair with mobility. Americans have the unique ability to go where they want when they want."

Indeed, Judy Wallerstein, 89, of Belvedere, California, who voluntarily turned in her keys last year, recalls driving for hours to get the exact type of coiffure she fancied.

"If Monsieur Pierre didn't cut my hair, life was not worth living," she declares. "In New York, you'd just walk down 57th Street. But this was in the Midwest, and if you wanted a French salon, if you wanted Monsieur Pierre, you had to drive 70 miles, and if it was tornado time, the hell with that – I had to get my hair done!"

Only in America!

And only in America would a young woman drop everything to take a 3,000-mile spin to assuage her lonely heart, as Mary Rogers did in April 1943, when her newlywed husband was summoned to naval duty on the other side of the country.

Rogers, now 94 and back in California, had just gotten her driver's license. She lost no time in subleasing the couple's apartment in Beverly Hills, persuading another "deserted" military bride to join her, plopping a bag of belongings in a 1938 Ford and setting off for Camp Peary near Williamsburg, Virginia, to be with her man.

She had a map from the American Automobile Association and some basic directions from her uncle to guide her.

"My uncle trained me to change a tire and put the towing rope on the car," Rogers recalls. "He told me what I was supposed to do, because he was the only one with a car. My father never had one."

Rogers and her traveling companion, Laura, headed out on the old U.S. Route 66, fabled in song and a television series. Starting in Los Angeles, they rolled through Pasadena, climbed the San Gabriel Mountains and crossed the Mojave Desert.

"As we ascended the mountain, the little car would get hot and boil. I would pull to the side of the road. No trucker would ever pass me without stopping and coming back and asking, 'Are you in trouble?' 'No, I don't think I'm in trouble, I just have to cool off my car,' I'd respond. 'Okay, I'll stay with you until your car is cooled,' he'd invariably insist."

The California girls had at least three such encounters with the road cowboys before reaching Prescott, Arizona, their first stop.

"It's no wonder," Rogers asserts. "There were two of us in our little car, both gorgeous, young, fresh. By the time we got to Prescott, Laura had had it. 'I'm going to take the next train home,' she informed me. 'I'm going on,' I persisted, reminding her we decided to go to Virginia to be with our husbands. A lot of women were doing that."

No teetotaler in those days, Rogers confides that "at least a couple of martinis would set you up for the evening. Or bourbon."

"After she had her first two drinks," she recounts, "Laura decided she would go on after all."

The next day, the pair journeyed ahead to Albuquerque, New Mexico. "We got a motel room and decided to have a drink. There was no bar at the motel, so we had to go around the corner and down a side alley to some hole-in-the-wall. We walked in, and of course we're the only women there, and all we see are Indians and a lot of cowboys. We bought a pint of bourbon and scampered back to the motel to have our drinks and go to sleep."

But sleep they could not, because continuous crashing and banging kept jarring them awake.

"It turned out the motel was less than half a mile from the railroad tracks, and during the night they were moving all these trains around. Crash! Crash! The horrible part about it was that the next morning we drove just a little bit farther and beheld this grand, beautiful, quiet hotel with bars and everything we could possibly want!"

As they proceeded, the radiator boiled over once again, requiring Rogers to pull off the rain-soaked road.

"I realized if I tried to get out, I would skid in the mud," she recalls. "We're sitting there, wondering what to do, when here comes a truck driver. [He] stops, backs up, and asks the usual, 'Can I help you?' This time, I exclaim, 'Yes, you sure can!' So he pulls out the tow rope my uncle had tossed in, tows us out of the muck, says goodbye, and we're on our way again."

It was a time, Rogers reminisces, when "all across the country, everyone helped everyone. If you saw a sailor or somebody on the road, you picked him up. No questions asked."

It was also a time of spring showers and flooded roadways, which periodically impeded their progress.

"We're trying to get into Nashville," Rogers remembers. "The roads are not good, so I decide to find the Greyhound bus station, and where the bus goes I will go. If a bus can get there, I can get there. That got us to the next place and the next."

Nearing Tennessee, they stopped at a motel for the night.

"I see all these Army cars around and think they would make a good escort. So, at 5 o'clock in the morning, we are up, and as soon as these Army cars start to move, we are right in with them. We're heading to a bivouac encampment, an area where they are training soldiers to live in tents in the desert. The next morning there are all these tents with all the guys waking up. And here are these two women, gorgeous of course, getting up with them!"

Continuing eastward, they encountered more flooding. At one point, they had to wait several hours for the military men to construct a floating bridge so they could cross a river into Virginia. "We stopped at Roanoke to spend the night at a bed and breakfast. We were dead tired, and the people were so good to us. The next day, we were going to Williamsburg to see our husbands, and this wonderful woman said, 'You've got to bathe and have your hair washed.' She fed us and gave us a comfortable bed, and got us up in the morning and made sure we were presentable for our husbands."

By this time the Ford had blown a muffler, noisily announcing their arrival.

"The roads into Williamsburg were brick, making the bang! bang! bang! Quite pronounced," Rogers says, blushing at the memory. The embarrassing racket was forgotten, however, when she beheld "my handsome Cam Rogers standing on the curb! He got a room for us for that night. It was quite some night!"

Such stories abound in the annals of the American road. The automobile has carried millions of Americans through much of life's journey – from the birthing center to the final resting place and many of the major stops in between.

"We do have a love affair with the automobile that's extended for generations, and I don't see anything in the trends that shows this will change," says Max Gurwell, veteran Ohio state patrolman, founder of Keeping Us Safe, a national group serving senior drivers, and author of Beyond Driving with Dignity: The Workbook for the Families of Older Drivers.

In some instances, cars become part of the family, marvels Charley Fenner, head of the California DMV's advocacy program for seniors.

"We give them names and even assign personalities to them; we become attached to them because they represent so much of our own personalities. They ... give us a mobile sanctuary, and they are symbols of hope, because as long as we have a car we have independence."

Accordingly, the first car, even if borrowed, initiates the rite of passage to adulthood, freeing adolescents from their reliance on others for getting around, pulling them away from parents and pushing them toward life on their own.

"Driving is really the first grownup thing kids get to do," observes Dr. Donald J. Iverson, a physician with the Humboldt Neurological Medical Group, Inc., in Eureka, California.

"Obviously, that's associated with a huge amount of independence," adds the father of four teenagers, the youngest one newly licensed, "with gaining responsibility and leaving childhood behind."

Wallerstein, a retired psychology professor at the University of California, Berkeley, puts part of the blame for Americans' car fixation from the earliest age on a deliberate marketing scheme by auto advertisers, who stoke the symbolic significance of driving as an essential step into young adulthood.

Be that as it may, the need for personal transportation in areas with limited mass transit, such as Marin County where she resides, undeniably exists. That need becomes acutely felt at the other end of the age spectrum, where the process of youthful slipping into the driver's seat shifts into reverse.

"For seniors, mobility is more than just a convenience; it is a quality-of-life issue," Locher emphasizes. "For seniors, mobility means independence, socialization and security."

Take away the car, and in too many cases you lose all three. No wonder retirement from driving, especially if forced, can lead to isolation, loneliness, depression, dependence and even a shortened lifespan. [12]

The key to avoiding such hazards is to prepare early for the end of the road, participate in activities and programs that can prolong safe driving, and persevere in seeing the light at the end of the tunnel – even from the passenger's seat. [13]

"Age isn't the issue, ability is," says Fenner, who continues to drive at 73. "We should begin to prepare for the inevitable, based on our health, mental status, financial status and skills."

"Most of us plan where to live based on price, crime, neighborhoods, schools and other considerations," he adds. But how many of us "buy a house, rent a condo or otherwise move to an area because 'in 10 years I won't be able to drive, and this location has a plethora of mobility options for seniors?'"

Deterioration in physical, medical, mental, visual and skill acuity should start turning the thought process toward that transition, he recommends. If your health is holding up, you should begin planning for your retirement from the road at the same time you start strategizing about your exit from the workforce.

Rogers, who spent years as a financial consultant and wrote two best-selling books on the topic following her romantic road trip, thinks independent-minded drivers should initiate a plan of action even sooner: with their first paycheck.

"They should never spend all of their income," she insists.

Having followed that dictum, Rogers had saved enough to afford the help required to stay on her own when she decided to stop driving at age 88.

"A part of that income has to be put away," she asserts. It will be needed to remain independent after the car keys are laid to rest. Those who would like to postpone that day might want to participate in activities aimed at extending their road life.

Numerous organizations, including AARP and the American Automobile Association, hold mature-driver classes that focus on age-related physical and mental changes affecting road skill and safety. As an added bonus, course completion may trigger discounts in insurance premiums. [14, 15]

As you will read, we offer important tips along those lines within these pages, courtesy of our resident editor and safe-driving author Phil Berardelli.

Various groups periodically sponsor special events and publish materials with the seasoned driver in mind. For instance, the American Society on Aging created CarFit, a free, 12-point checkup for a better and safer match between vehicles and operators past their 50th birthday. One item calls for checking hand placement on the steering wheel, which today's experts position at 9 o'clock and 3 o'clock, in contrast to the formerly recommended 10 and 2, to which most senior drivers still adhere.

The California DMV's Senior Guide for Safe Driving suggests a number of devices to make cars more senior-driver-friendly, including large side or panoramic mirrors, power steering, turning knobs instead of pushbuttons, seat-belt adaptors, and pedal extenders.

Those with physical disabilities can benefit from sessions with an occupational therapist, although few of these experts specialize in driving and many charge hefty fees, which most insurance policies fail to cover, Fenner notes. Nevertheless, the DMV contends, occupational and physical therapists along with driver rehabilitation specialists "can put you back in the driver's seat or keep you there."

Other options include assistive technologies, a field expanding as quickly as the number of drivers 65 and older, expected to pass the 40-million mark in less than a decade.[16]

John Matras, our resident auto writer, covers this area in an upcoming chapter.

"New technologies are evolving so rapidly that evidence demonstrating their impact on driving skills and safety sometimes lags behind development," cautions Virginia G. Wadley, associate professor of medicine at the University of Alabama at Birmingham.

"Some technologies, such as the GPS (Global Positioning System), can present a distraction that poses a safety risk unless used appropriately," states Wadley, who also is director of the university's Dementia Care Research Program in the Division of Gerontology, Geriatrics and Palliative Care as well as associate director of the Edward R. Roybal Center for Translational Research on Aging and Mobility.

On the neurological side, an array of computer-based training programs, many available through auto insurance companies, aims to boost cognitive functions that affect driving, such as focusing and information processing.[17]

The best selections cite studies published in peer-reviewed scientific journals, Wadley advises. Whatever the choice in external tools, she adds, getting adequate sleep, monitoring the side effects of medications and otherwise leading a healthy lifestyle also can prolong one's driving days.

Computer-savvy seniors can navigate the information superhighway for points of interest, such as the California DMV's award-winning Web site, which highlights a special senior section. Among other features, it presents five practice license-renewal tests.

In addition, the agency's Senior Driver Ombudsman Program, the only one of its kind in the nation, offers assistance at every turn.

"We work with the development of legislation relating to senior mobility, and we help individual seniors," explains Fenner, the SDOP's chief, who is featured in the program's informational video. "The senior driver ombudsmen are members on more than a dozen state, federal and local task forces specific to senior driving and mobility."

Their achievements include production of a pamphlet titled "Preparing for Your Supplemental Driving Performance Evaluation," which specifies the skills required to pass the exam and keep on trucking in safety.

At some point, age-related changes in body and/or mind may start affecting those skills and serve as warning signs of possible danger ahead.

3. Autonomy

by Robert A. Comunale, M.D.

I didn't do it. Nobody saw me do it. There's no way you can prove anything!

— Bart Simpson

Strange as it may seem, famous young bad-boy Bart's assertions pretty much reflect what the elderly tend to express when confronted with the results of a mishap, whether it's an accidental puddle of urine, a broken dish, a burnt pot on the stove or … a vehicular crash. They adopt an amazed look of innocence and a defiant posture of denial.

Such was my encounter with a couple who arrived at my office one day preceded by the unmistakable sound of metal violently compressing metal.

"Dr. Comunale, the Weintraubs are here."

It was my last appointment before catching up on charts and heading out for hospital rounds. The Weintraubs – naturally, not their real name – were a new family referred to me by one of my old classmates who had long ago established a practice in New York State. They moved to Northern Virginia to settle in one of the affluent retirement communities springing up around the area.

"Barbara, Virginia, what was that noise?"

My two secretaries stared at me. Virginia, in my employ for over three decades, just shook her head.

"Your car bumper being crushed," she replied, as a couple in their late 60s walked into the reception room.

"Dr. Comunale?"

"Mr. Weintraub?"

"Uh … yes, sorry about that. Is that your car?"

"It is."

"My wife needs a lot of room to park. You shouldn't leave your car like that."

My old red Jeep was in its usual corner, out of the way of everything – except Mrs. Weintraub.

I stuck to the matter at hand.

"What can we do for you today, Mr. Weintraub?"

"My wife's getting a bit forgetful. Got any magic pills for her?"

We sat in an examining room while I took a medication history: heart meds, sleeping pills, anti-anxiety medication, muscle relaxants, cholesterol-lowering drugs, anti-hypertension meds – those were the prescription drugs. Then came the bag of herbals and other remedies.

I examined Rachel Weintraub. A pleasant woman who smiled nonstop, she could tell me all about the old neighborhood in New York but couldn't remember her new address here.

I observed other characteristics as well. Her gait – the way she walked – was hesitant. There was a tremor in her hands.

"Mr. Weintraub, your wife has quite a few problems, not the least of which is the number of medications she's taking. We need to work on reducing or eliminating the drugs that are decreasing her ability to function clearly."

Then came the part I dreaded.

"I'm afraid she shouldn't be driving. With her problems, she's a danger to herself and others."

I could tell by the instant expression change that this was a non-starter.

"What? Doctor, you're crazy if you think I'm going to take her keys away. She's not even 70 yet!"

He rose, took his wife's hand and helped her to her feet.

"I'll leave our insurance information with your secretary when we pay the bill," he told me, as they walked out of the examining room.

"Your usual tact, Dr. C.?" Barbara, my other secretary, asked a few minutes later.

"I told them that Mrs. Weintraub shouldn't drive anymore."

"You should have enlisted the help of their kids," she said.

As always, she was right.

We go through life yearning to be free. From the time we proudly hoist ourselves upright, usually to the beaming approval of our parents, to the time we get our first set of wheels – be they on a tricycle, a bicycle, or our first automobile, the thrust is always toward freedom of motion and activity.

But inevitably, physiology takes over.

Let's consider how advancing age can affect our five primary senses: sight, hearing, smell, taste and touch.

Sight

By our early to mid-40s, the ability of the eye's lens to contract or expand, which allows us to focus near and far, begins to decline. We find ourselves holding newspapers at arm's length and cringing when the eye doctor asks us if we want separate reading glasses or bifocals.

Genetics and medications also come into play.

If your parents experienced early onset of cataracts, or clouding of the lenses, you will likely develop them, too.

The pressure inside the eye may also begin to rise. Glaucoma, either an overproduction of fluid or an increased blockage of normal outflow channels within the eye, can cause silent and gradual destruction of the optic nerve at the back of the eyeball, subsequently decreasing vision.

If you find yourself admiring mystical halos around street lights at night, get checked for cataracts and/or glaucoma. If you notice that you no longer see things on each side, but only in a narrow "tunnel" view, get checked fast!

As we age, we need more external help to correct imbalances in body chemistries and function. These medications have prolonged life and meaningful function far past prior generations. But there is a price to pay.

Cholesterol-lowering drugs have helped to cut back heart and brain dysfunctions, but the so-called statins can create a side effect: early cataract formation.

Other heart drugs such as digoxin – aka a synthetic form of digitalis – can cause changes in color perception.

As any man who has tried what we euphemistically call "the little blue pill" to "restore his vigor" can tell you, the medication can affect red and blue color vision.

You might ask why that's a driving-related problem, especially when it allows you to act like a newlywed again. If so, remind yourself about the three colors of traffic signals.

Color vision isn't trivial, but for seniors it's a side issue. At the top of the list is the most insidious change in eyesight: macular degeneration, which causes blurred vision, wavy lines, a progressive inability to see small objects and read text, and emerging gaps in the field of vision.

Hold up your hand, close one eye and look at your hand. Do you see the entire hand? When you look at an object, do you see the middle part?

Macular degeneration destroys the most sensitive part of the eye: the retina.

Picture a TV screen with a hole in the middle. The TV screen in our eyes, the retina, is made up of millions of tiny cells that allow us to see shades of black and white.

But in the very center is a spot that contains an even higher density of cells. Those cells allow us to see fine details and colors. Damage that tiny spot and our central, detailed vision is gone.

Yes, there are some techniques that can stop the regression, but nothing so far totally reverses the loss of those macular cells.

Visit any retirement center or nursing home and the most common complaint you'll encounter, aside from bladder dysfunction, is decreasing ability to read.

State motor vehicle departments throughout the country recognize the rising percentage of older drivers experiencing visual difficulties.

Loss of peripheral vision – tunnel vision – is a common cause of auto accidents, particularly when seniors attempt to make left turns out of driveways or at intersections.

Evening and night accidents rise because of the distortions caused by glaucoma, cataracts or loss of central acute vision.

State and federal laws require more frequent vision testing as we age, and DMVs have set vision standards that require mandatory restrictions.

If you have monocular vision, meaning you've lost sight in one eye, but you can still maintain 20/20 corrected vision – via glasses – in the other eye, there is no restriction. But if the one good eye cannot be corrected below 20/70 – requiring you to stand 20 feet away to see something that someone with 20/20 can see at 70 feet – you will not be allowed to drive at night. If your vision is not correctable below 20/1000, you are considered legally blind and cannot drive at all.

Hearing

"Quit mumbling, damn it! I can't understand a word you're saying."

How many wives have heard those angry words from their spouse?

Surprising, but diminished hearing is not considered a limitation to driving.

My personal opinion? Senior citizens need every bit of sensory input to drive safely.

The National Highway Traffic Safety Administration states that nearly one-third of drivers over the age of 65 have some form of hearing loss.

Think about it: you are bopping along the highway and you don't hear the ambulance siren, the fire truck's klaxon or the dreaded police horn. You don't hear the honking horns of drivers who want to pass you or the rumbling of giant tractor trailers riding your bumper.

Numerous articles give tips on how to beat the system if you have hearing loss, but there are no specific requirements or limitations if you can't.

Taste and Smell

Not an issue – unless your car is on fire or leaking gas. However, if you have a loss of taste or smell – and taste is in large part controlled by smell – you may have an obstruction in your nasal passages that diminishes oxygen flow to the lungs.

Just a thought.

Proprioception

What an important sounding word to describe our ability to feel things and keep our balance.

Driving proprioception: You put your hands on the steering wheel. You feel the vibration of the car engine. You step out, or into, your car and know where your feet are going.

As we age, changes in our bodies due to heredity, diabetes, neurologic diseases, and just plain wear and tear from time affect the nerve endings and special sensors in our skin that tell the brain "hot, cold, rough, sharp, uneven" just don't function as well

The primary cause is diabetes – it is not just a "sugar" disease.

Imbalances in our body's ability to handle sugars and fats causes damage to nerves which carry those messages. Arteries that feed nerve cells become damaged.

We get tingling in our feet and hands called mononeuritis multiplex. Yes, it's quite a mouthful of words, but you would do well to learn about it, because it can damage the arteries and nerves in our eyes, located in the retina – that TV screen of the brain.

Reflexes are slowed. We see the teenager weaving in and out of traffic but don't respond as quickly to his erratic moves given our diminished response time. We walk a bit unsteadily, our legs slightly wider apart like a tripod to keep our balance, because the bottoms of our feet are becoming numb.

Try feathering the gas pedal or the brake if you can't feel them.

The Ol' CPU

So far we have mentioned the peripheral sensors that give us feedback to our world. All those billions of bits of information need to be processed by our built-in computer, the hardware we call the brain.

The brain has two major functions: cognitive and motor.

Cognitive: Cogito ergo sum. I think, therefore I am – thanks to René Descartes.

Who we are – our personality, our behavioral idiosyncrasy – boils down to a bunch of electrical impulses bouncing back and forth within certain parts of our brain.

No, I won't discuss the soul. Leave that to theologians, though even the most devout atheist might be heard to utter a prayer – if not a profanity – on the cusp of a collision. For our purposes, it means that damage to certain brain areas causes changes in personality.

Even the Nazis knew it: Stick a needle under the upper eyelid, puncture the bone, move the needle back and forth like a car windshield wiper and, voila! You've created a human being who has no social restraints. He pees on the front lawn, says exactly what he thinks no matter the audience and won't hesitate to perform unpleasantries in public.

The Nazis performed frontal lobotomies on thousands of unfortunate souls.

In a sense, time does the same to us.

Stroke, the sudden rupture or blockage of an artery by a clot, can destroy parts of the brain critical to rational thought. It can be sudden and massive, in which case the person usually dies, or it can impose a "ratchet" effect.

The brain has large, medium and small arteries. Over a period of time the tiniest vessels can block, cutting off the blood that carries food and oxygen to a small number of cells. They die but we continue to function, unaware of their loss.

Now, picture clusters of small arteries shutting down and clusters of cells dying. Gradually the function in that area decreases in ratchet fashion. If it occurs in the frontal, parietal and temporal lobes, our judgment diminishes.

"Grandma was so good a year ago. Now, every month she seems to slip downhill a bit."

Mini-strokes—or Alzheimer's?

Deposits of amyloid and Tau protein in the neuron endings that process memory and judgment can cause a gradual deterioration of both functions. Initial symptoms may be nothing more than an increase in "senior moments," those instances where thoughts seem to jump out of your head with lightning speed.

As time progresses, however, such memory gaps can cause growing confusion and agitation, and they can lead to a living death, in which the body survives but the personality that once inhabited it does not.

One of those fun statistical studies that people enjoy as much as TV reality shows claims that, by the time we hit our 80s, we all will show "slippage" in the memory-retrieval area. But there is help. The Franklin Institute has created a regimen of "brain-retraining" exercises to help strengthen your memory and slow its deterioration.

Motor Skills

We sit, stand, walk, run, laugh, cry, make love – all of which require our voluntary and involuntary muscles to be in good working order.

The brain sends a message: "Get off your butt and put the garbage out."

No, wait, that's your wife saying that. But your brain still directs your muscles to get up and do it.

But cut off the blood supply to the motor area of the brain and say bye-bye to movement. Or, damage a part of the base of the brain that controls balance and you need the assistance of a third leg: a cane, a walker, etc.

Even arthritis can play a part.

Narrowing of the bony canal through which the nerves travel from the brain can cause dysfunction in our abilities to walk and move our arms. When arthritis becomes severe enough in the neck, just turning your head from side to side can cut off the blood flow to the brain and cause loss of consciousness.

Remember that statistic about auto accidents and senior citizens making left hand turns?

Mixed Neurology
We're talking about Parkinsonism.

Remember Muhammad Ali, né Cassius Clay?

Too many hits to the head damaged a central area of Ali's brain called the basal ganglia. Now it no longer produces key chemicals that control the nerves that prevent his arms and legs from shaking.

Unfortunately, the disease can also cause dementia similar to Alzheimer's.

The Wonderful One-Horse Shay
In Oliver Wendell Holmes's poem The Deacon's Masterpiece, the deacon in question attempts to construct a horse-drawn shay so well that it will last forever.

Most of us harbor similar thoughts about our bodies.

At present, we actually can – partially – reduce age-related changes, as least for a while. But heredity, the chance flip of the dice in which we inherit both good and bad genes, sets us up for changes in our bodies that are different from what another person experiences.

One person remains alert and active until he dies in his sleep at 100. Another dies at 45 of sudden irregular heartbeats – just like his or her father or mother.

Don't believe the claims made for nutritional supplements that promise to make you function like a 20 year old. For one thing, they might lead to a stroke or heart attack.

Heart Disease
Narrowing of the heart valves, especially the aortic and mitral valves, can cause syncope, or the sudden loss of consciousness.

So, too, can sudden irregular heartbeats.

Atrial fibrillation can cause clots to form in the upper chamber of the heart that break loose, travel to the brain, and cause strokes. Unfortunately, the drugs used to control heartbeats and give strength to weakened heart muscle have their own effects on judgment and consciousness.

Have a pacemaker or implanted pacemaker/defibrillator?

You're driving along when your heart suddenly decides to do a rumba dance. Your pacemaker kicks in and, if the beat is especially irregular, the defibrillator as well, your chest feels like a mule just kicked it.

You might double over, lose control of the steering wheel or pass out. In other words, you crash, maybe killing others in your car or someone else's car.

What about Mr. and Mrs. Weintraub?

My secretaries were right again.

I contacted their offspring, Ben, Judith and Abe, and described my findings and concerns. They then spoke at length with Sol and even traveled to Virginia to observe their mother. As a result they took the driver's license from Rachel's purse and returned it to the motor vehicle department.

Rachel Weintraub: Some of her symptoms were medication in-duced, but the signs of Alzheimer's in the absence of other meta-bolic causes confirmed the diagnosis. She was also in early stage Parkinsonism.

Neither Sol nor his wife ever spoke to me again. Their insur-ance company did repair my car, however. I would have been lost without my "wheels."

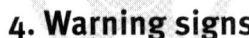

4. Warning signs

by Lidia Wasowicz Pringle

What's a senior? You get quite a different answer, depending on whom you ask: movie theaters, airlines, ski resorts, parks, bus companies – all of which give "senior" discounts at different ages – life insurance plans, corporations, municipal, state and federal governments, which calculate benefits [based] on a different retirement age. There needs to be a consensus in answering that question before enacting any rules, regulations, limitations and/or policies relating to something as crucial to independent living as driving.

– Joy B., 63

To avoid injury or death, all safety-conscious drivers take careful notice of the vividly colored or brightly illuminated traffic signs warning of approaching hazards, be they hairpin turns on narrow mountain roads or patches of black ice on slippery winter streets.

In similar fashion and for the same reason, drivers need to pay attention to less clear-cut but equally critical clues to physical and/or mental shifts that come with age and could portend some major changes in driving status.

Speaking loosely, the human body, like the car's, wears and tears through life's bumpy ride, its deterioration highly individualized and dependent in part on the care it receives and the quality of the original construction. Spare parts and repair can provide a fix – albeit a temporary one. When the final warranty expires, retirement from the road may remain the only option to keep the costs in safety at an acceptable level.

That option gains traction with age, research indicates, with one study of adults 50 and older estimating that the average man will outlive his ability to drive by six years; the average woman by as much as a decade. [18]

As Dr. Comunale has described, the main components that tend to fail over time include sight, hearing, reflexes, strength, flexibility and cognition – particularly memory. In addition, a general decline in health, and side effects from certain medications, can bear adversely on a driver's fitness to stay behind the wheel. [19, 20]

Those in shape to drive possess vision acute enough to read road signs, judge distances, spot danger in various light conditions and adjust to traffic flow. They also boast a mind sharp enough to juggle multiple messages simultaneously, maintain focus for prolonged periods and respond quickly to any unforeseen circumstances. Their bodies remain nimble enough to react swiftly in an emergency. Their neck retains sufficient flexibility to turn the head over the shoulder for backing or changing lanes, and their arm and leg muscles flex with adequate strength for steering, slowing and speeding up, according to those who set such requirements. [21]

Of course, these standards apply to all age groups, and youth does not confer automatic immunity against diseases, disorders and disabilities that could compromise them. Poor eyesight, impaired hearing or lost use of an arm are not confined to mature drivers, stresses Norman Abeles, past president of the American Psychological Association and professor of psychology at Michigan State University in East Lansing.

"Should people with an IQ of 80 be allowed to drive?" asks Abeles, who specializes in aging issues. "How about an IQ of 75? How about driving for the illiterate? Frankly, I do not think there is such a thing as being too old to drive," he says.

At least one centenarian agrees. Washington, D.C., resident Mary E. Cooper, who turned 101 recently and still drives, told a local newspaper columnist that "it's your health that matters, not your age." [22]

Abeles has taken the words right out of the American Medical Association's mouthpiece on the topic, the Physician's Guide to Assessing and Counseling Older Drivers, presented in collaboration with the National Highway Traffic Safety Administration.

"Please note that age alone is not a red flag!" the nation's largest doctor group urges practitioners, decrying the pervasive "ageism" that tempts news reporters to zero in on senior drivers who mess up. [23]

"While many people experience a decline in vision, cognition or motor skills as they get older, people age at different rates and experience functional changes to different degrees," the AMA states. "The focus should be on functional abilities and medical fitness to drive and not on age per se." [24]

The physician is directed to be on the alert for any condition, medication or symptom that could affect driving skills. Typically, this list will lengthen as time goes by. [25]

"A lot of medical conditions that affect how well and safely we drive have a general incidence that increases with age," says Dr. Donald J. Iverson, the neurologist and country doctor from Eureka, California.

These include dementia, diabetes, hypertension, sleep apnea, ocular problems, musculoskeletal diseases such as arthritis, stroke, and Parkinson's disease, and excessive use of medications and alcohol.

"The longer you're around," Iverson observes, "the more likely something's going to get you."

It could be slower reflexes, limited neck mobility, vision loss, or neuropathy related to diabetes, among other conditions, says Virginia G. Wadley, the geriatrics specialist at the University of Alabama at Birmingham.

"As we age, we all tend to slow down in our ability to process the information we can perceive in a single glance while driving," she notes. "We may misjudge the speed or distance of oncoming traffic when making an unprotected left turn; among older adults this is one of the most common situations in which a crash occurs."

That sums up the experience of Max Gurwell during his 24 years on the Ohio State Highway Patrol. "When I talk to older drivers," says Gurwell, whose workshops and workbook, *Beyond Driving with Dignity; The workbook for the families of older drivers*, help senior drivers stay on the road safely and, should the time come, retire with minimal distress, "I tell them, 'If you learn anything from this talk, be careful about left-hand turns because that's likely to be your demise.'"

Mistaking the gas and brake pedals, and misjudging the force to apply to either, also rank among the "senior moments" that may throw mature drivers in harm's way.

"One of the problems I've observed with senior drivers is many can't sense the bottom of their feet," says Judy Mark, the doctor's daughter who learned to drive at her father's side.

Unable to feel the pedals, they may apply too much pressure when they hit the gas. Or they may slam on the brakes. The result: "a lot of jarring stop-starts, which I especially notice when a friend who shall remain nameless drives on the highway," Mark confides. "She's had several accidents running into fences because she was pressing too hard, going too fast and suddenly had to find the brakes."

Among the changes associated with advancing years, vision can weaken due to a variety of factors, including cataracts, glaucoma, macular degeneration and physiological adjustments that shift color perception, limit side vision, decrease clarity and make it difficult to see in the dark, up close and in the glare of headlights, sunshine or street lamps. Dwindling sight stands out as a top reason for seniors to have their licenses restricted or revoked. [26]

To see if you're at risk for either, you can take any number of tests and self-assessments, many available online. One, offered by NHTSA, aims to help you keep tabs on and adapt to any developments that might compromise road safety. [27]

Here's a portion:
1. How is your eyesight? Do you have trouble...
Reading signs easily?
Recognizing someone you know from across the street?
Seeing street markings, other cars and people walking – especially at dawn, dusk and at night?
Handling headlight glare at night?

If you answered "Yes" to any of these questions, you should:

Make sure you always wear your glasses and that the prescription is current.

Keep your windshield, mirrors and headlights clean.

Make sure that your headlights are working and aimed correctly.

Sit high enough in your seat so you can see the road for at least 10 feet in front of your vehicle.

If you are 60 or older, see an eye doctor every year.

2. Do you have control of your vehicle? Loss of strength, coordination and flexibility can make it hard to control. Do you have trouble...

Looking over your shoulder to change lanes?

Moving your foot from the gas to the brake pedal?

Turning the steering wheel?

Walking less than a block a day?

Going up or down stairs because you have pain in your knees, legs or ankles?

If you answered "Yes" to any of these questions, you should:

Know that an automatic transmission, power steering and brakes and other special equipment can make it easier for you to drive your vehicle and use the foot pedals.

Check with your doctor about physical therapy, medicine, stretching exercises or a walking or fitness program.

Reduce your driver's-side blind spot by moving your mirrors.

Watch for flashing lights of emergency vehicles.

Listen for sounds outside your vehicle.

3. Does driving make you feel nervous, scared or overwhelmed? Do you...

Feel confused by traffic signs and people and cars in traffic?

Take medicine that makes you sleepy?

Get dizzy or have seizures or losses of consciousness?

React slowly to normal driving situations?

If you answered "Yes" to any of these questions, you should:
Ask your doctor if your health or side effects from your medicine can affect your driving.

Take routes that you know.

Try to drive during the day (avoid rush hour).

Keep a safe distance between you and the car ahead of you.

Always scan the road while you are driving so that you are ready for any problems and can plan your actions.

4. Are loved ones concerned? Sometimes other people notice things about your driving that you might have missed. Have people you know and trust told you they are concerned about your driving? If you answered "Yes," you should:
Talk with your doctor. Ask him or her to check the side effects of any medicines you are taking.

Think about taking a mature-driving class. The AAA, AARP and driving schools offer these classes.

Try walking, carpooling [or using] public transit and other forms of alternative transportation. [28]

In addition to following such suggestions, many drivers respond to the changes they experience by altering their driving habits.

"They realize their reflexes aren't as quick as they used to be; that's why they don't drive on the freeway, that's why they drive a bit slower," observes John D. Locher, the senior-driver ombudsman at the California DMV. "They become tired more easily so they don't drive on long trips, or, if they do, they schedule rest stops. We younger drivers tend to push our limits and drive tired on long trips."

The AMA also takes note of this self-restricting tendency in its handbook for assessing older drivers:

"In 1990, males over 70 drove on average 8,298 miles, compared with 16,784 miles for men 20 to 24; for women, the figures were 3,976 miles and 11,807 miles, respectively." Mature adults also are more likely to wear seat belts and avoid such risky behaviors as speeding, tailgating, and drinking and driving. [29]

"Older drivers not only drive substantially less but also tend to modify when and how they drive," the AMA reports. "When they recognize loss of ability to see well after dark, many stop driving at night. There are data that suggest older women are more likely to self-regulate than men. Others who understand the complex demands of left turns at uncontrolled intersections – and their own diminished capacity – forgo left-hand turns and make a series of right turns instead." [30]

Such self-awareness and restraint may suffice among "cognitively intact" seniors to judge their continued fitness to drive. [31]

What about those who aren't cognitively intact?

Impairments in cognition – the scientific term for the brain's processing of information, such as awareness, perception, memory, reasoning, judgment, learning and problem-solving – take a toll on driving, which at any age requires highly honed mental skills, including focus and visual interpretation. [32]

Among other factors, disease and decay can cause neurological disarray that could make driving a risky business.

"Our brains continue to grow until early adulthood," explains Kirk Erickson, assistant professor of psychology at the University of Pittsburgh and lead author of a study linking physical exercise to cognitive health in older adults. "Once we reach late adulthood, our brains begin to decay. This growth and decay are probably important factors in determining our driving abilities." [33]

Neurological disorders that can blindside cognition and waylay driving skills include brain tumors, multiple sclerosis, Parkinson's disease, seizures, stroke, sleep abnormalities, vertigo and dementia. [34]

Often unrecognized and undocumented during the early stages, when treatment might slow its progress, dementia casts a devastating shadow over the minds it methodically destroys. Susceptibility to the brain disorder, which affects as many as 6.8 million Americans, increases with age. [35]

"Its incidence in the 65-to-74 age group is 2.5 percent," reports Iverson, lead author of new American Academy of Neurology guidelines on "Driving and Dementia," which allows the driver's-side door to remain open for seniors with mild impairment. "Among people over 85, up to half the population has dementia."

The most common cause of the disintegration of intellectual faculties, Alzheimer's disease affects one-third of those past their 80th birthday, Iverson says.

Unlike the self-regulating motorists with physical limitations, those with mental debilities tend to show little restraint, often leaving the tough task of rescinding their driving privileges to family and caregivers. [36]

In an analysis of 27 studies, researchers report that one-third of patients seen at a dementia clinic had had a car accident since their first symptoms appeared. [37]

"The 'change' that invariably affects driving adversely is a dementia, such as Alzheimer's disease," says Wadley, an expert in the field. "At the earliest stages, one may be able to compensate for dementia-related losses by limiting one's driving to familiar routes and avoiding challenging situations, such as driving at night, during rush hour, or in bad weather. When dementia reaches moderate severity, driving must stop."

Alzheimer's and its ilk affect both behavior and thinking, making short shrift of the extended focus required behind the wheel. [38]

Dementia may increase the difficulty of performing the crucial cerebral chore of plucking significant signals from a sea of stimuli vying for the driver's attention. [39]

That task is tough enough for intellectually intact older individuals, according to research that suggests the capability to distinguish between important and irrelevant information in transit fades over time. [40]

Counterintuitive as it may seem, the characteristic develops because the ability to take in the entire moving picture actually improves with age. Detected in all test participants older than 64, and in some as young as 60, the astute awareness of background motion runs the risk of overloading the brain with needless input, making it more difficult to discern critical, up-front moving targets, such as pedestrians, cyclists and cars, the study authors conclude. [41]

"This may sound like a good thing for older adults, but if presented with a highly dynamic visual scene (such as during driving), suppression of often irrelevant background motions is advantageous," says study leader Dr. Duje Tadin, professor of brain and cognitive sciences at the University of Rochester in New York. "Basically, this is one more thing that makes driving harder as we age."

The investigators traced the problematic phenomenon to a brain area that, when working properly in healthy young people, puts the brakes on processing immaterial goings-on, facilitating focus on more relevant happenings. [42]

"Knowing this, we better understand how older adults perceive motion – a critical thing in driving," Tadin says. He anticipates the results might lead to training techniques that help those of advancing years advance their driving skills.

His team is conducting studies to determine whether practice makes perfect. Results thus far point in a positive direction, with older adults warming up over time to a task that initially stopped them cold: detecting moving objects on moving backgrounds.

"Our hypothesis is that they get better because they get better at suppressing distracting background motion," Tadin surmises.

In addition, the research is shedding light on the underlying neurochemistry that, once understood, could provide a basis for developing pharmacological aids, he proposes.

The work also points to ways of improving certain practices that determine driving status.

"Generally speaking, currently used vision tests for driving are not a good way to asses visual abilities needed for driving," Tadin asserts. "Driving involves viewing dynamic visual stimuli and making reactions based on those dynamic stimuli. Knowing one's visual acuity tells you very little about those abilities (in fact, one can have poor visual acuity and still be good at seeing moving objects)."

"What current vision tests tell us," he continues, "is really how good one can be at reading traffic signs, which is an important aspect of driving – but not the only one we should care about."

If you care about why you can't remember where you parked your trusty automobile, a group of neuroscientists using cutting-edge imaging techniques might have a clue.

Their findings, published May 2011 in the Proceedings of the National Academy of Sciences, reveal the pathways to the hippocampus degrade over time, curtailing the amount of input relayed to the memory storehouse from the rest of the brain, and limiting the seahorse-shaped structure's ability to do its job. [43]

With older memories butting in and obstructing the process, the aging brain fails to file complete, up-to-the-minute reports. Then, when required to recollect the car's location or some other situation encountered in the past, it tends to call up reserves of previously stored data rather than file and retrieve the latest information.

Confusion ensues. [44]

The research opens the door to testing medications that might impede the deterioration and dysfunction, the scientists say, noting that success in trials with early Alzheimer's patients ultimately might put a dent in the escalating number of dementia cases.

On a more immediately positive note, Erickson and colleagues found that one year of walking around a track for 40 minutes a day, three times a week, increased the size of the hippocampus – and improved spatial memory – in older adults, suggesting even moderate aerobic exercise can turn back the clock for brain health. [45]

So, the next time you're feeling down, traipsing around in search of your misplaced vehicle, think of the upside: You might be tripping up Father Time –though his intentions are never clear.

"Some people age quite successfully while others go downhill rapidly," Erickson notes.

Judy Mark plays duplicate bridge with nonagenarians who drive and are "perfectly sharp and perfectly capable of managing a car." They number among the 3.1 million Californians between ages 65 and 99 who hold a driver's license, according to the DMV's chief senior-driver ombudsman, Charley Fenner.

As one of their advocates, Locher likes to quote the "old at 20, young at 90" adage.

"When I was in the Marine Corps, I was a regimental scout sniper; I could see a man on a hillside a mile away, and I could shoot that man," he recalls. "Today, at 51 years of age, I can't throw a dart at 15 feet without glasses."

"Is my loss of vision an age issue?" he wonders. "It's impossible to say because don't you know someone who wears glasses at 10 years old, 15 years old, 20 years old? Of course, you do. Conversely, don't you know folks in their 80s or 90s who still have 20/20 vision? You may not, but they are out there."

Exceptions notwithstanding, trends do pop up.

"Usually there is some decline happening by the mid-60s," Erickson reports, "but serious decline usually does not start showing itself until the late 60s or 70s."

In that age group, women generally exhibit more caution behind the wheel, but men drive more frequently, racking up a safety advantage that comes with extra practice, Wadley notes.

"Socioeconomic status comes into play, insofar as people with fewer resources may have less driving opportunity and less access to a vehicle in good operating condition," she adds.

They also may have less access to medical care that can help keep their bodies in good operating condition. As the AMA points out, doctors often can prolong their patients' road life by diagnosing and treating cataracts, glaucoma, macular degeneration, arthritis and other conditions that can spell an end to their driving days, and by stopping or switching medicines that cause sleepiness or otherwise impair skills needed to stay behind the wheel. [46]

"We're learning that several important lifestyle features are probably important in preventing decline," Erickson says. He includes eating healthy foods, remaining physically active throughout life and retaining a curiosity about the world.

So, rather than sit and watch the meter expire, geriatric specialists advise getting out and depositing a bit of effort, thereby buying yourself some extra time. Beef up your muscles by lifting boxes, water bottles, soup cans or any other portable weight. Tone your arms and hands by squeezing stuffed animals or rubber balls. Pump up your heart with a walk, swim, dance, trip to the mall or visit to the garden patch, or plunge into an aqua-aerobics class. [47]

To keep your brain in working order, give it a workout by taking on crossword puzzles, word or number games, playing cards, or participating in any number of other mental exercises. In fact, a recent study of 908 older drivers, with a mean age of 73.1, found those who underwent cognitive training for memory, reasoning or speed of processing caused half as many car crashes over a six-year period as those who did not. [48, 49]

As Phil Berardelli stresses in his driving tips for seniors, among the best ways to stay safe is to proceed with caution, keeping your eye out, casually but constantly, for warning signs that could spell danger ahead.

"The biggest red flag that driving may be impaired is involvement in traffic incidents – even in minor fender benders in which another vehicle is not involved," Wadley observes.

Iverson has arrived at similar conclusions.

"Crashes and citations are a more important indicator of unsafe-driving risk than dementia," he asserts. "People over 70 who have two or more tickets are at highest risk, even more so than 16-year-old boys."

Substantially curtailed driving likewise may portend problems for older drivers, perhaps because of the reduced practice time or because the cutback reflects their own recognition that their skills are shot, he adds.

"The magic number is 60 miles per week," Iverson reports. "Less than that is associated with unsafe driving."

Other noteworthy forewarnings include permanent cessation of driving at night or in inclement weather, along with aggressive or impulsive behavior. [50]

For Locher of the DMV, any of the following should be viewed as a flashing yellow caution sign:

Deterioration in vision, memory and/or extremity control and strength;

Unexplained dings and dents in the vehicle;

An increase in "near-miss" collisions;

Anger, depression, or sleep disorders;

Getting lost or being confused behind the wheel, and

Concerns expressed about your driving by friends, family, police, or doctors.

Among pages of guidelines for assessing older drivers in its 2010 handbook, the AMA advises physicians to watch for:

Poor hygiene, grooming and general personal care;

Difficulty with walking, getting in and out of chairs, and other mobility;

Problems with visual tasks, and

Lack of attention, loss of memory, and difficulty in oral expression or comprehension. [51]

Noting the disparate standards set by the state departments of motor vehicles for evaluating older drivers – which range from automatic license renewal to required road tests and mandatory vision exams starting at ages varying from 40 in Maryland to 80 in Florida and Virginia – Wadley applauds the medical association's efforts at uniformity. [52]

"The AMA guidelines are a step in the right direction," she says, noting that physicians often must pass judgment on driver safety and in some states are legally required to report conditions that may pose a risk, raising concerns about doctor-patient confidentiality.

Independent of the AMA and narrower in scope, the neurology academy has developed its own, science-based parameters for determining when patients with Alzheimer's and other dementias should stop driving. [53]

Six years in the making, based on a review of 6,000 scientific abstracts, and published in 2010, the updated guidebook takes a more accepting view of drivers with mild dementia than did its predecessor, which required three years and an analysis of 400 studies to complete.

"The academy has more sophisticated data-retrieval techniques than it did in 2000, when the guidelines said patients with mild dementia should not drive," lead author Iverson explains. "There are people who still have that opinion."

He sees the view as "a bit draconian," considering that the latest studies show up to 60 percent of motorists with mild dementia can pass the driving test. [54]

"This is not a black-and-white decision," Iverson asserts. "You do not go from competent directly to incompetent; you go to an area with shades of gray. The new guidelines are more nuanced."

They suggest considering a number of factors – the caregiver's concerns about driving, a history of accidents and tickets, scores on the so-called Clinical Dementia Rating scale, and incidents of aggressive driving or behavior – in assessing a driver's suitability to stay behind the wheel. [55]

"If you have dementia, you have to face the eventuality that you'll have to stop driving," Iverson says. "If you find these risk factors, it's time to have a family discussion."

During such talks, those with qualms about the older driver should be heeded, he advises. Research gives greatest credence to caregivers' anxieties, he notes, not as much to their assurances, and least of all to drivers' glowing self-appraisals. [56]

"Assessments that 'he's fine' are not a very reliable indicator of driving safety, perhaps because the family doesn't want to rat him out," Iverson explains. "The study validated that when caregivers have a concern about a patient's ability to drive, it's usually warranted."

Agreeing, the DMV's Fenner and Locher say they get a lot of mileage out of interviews with friends and family, especially the senior driver's adult children.

"They are probably the best to communicate and observe the questionable driving," Locher says. He listens carefully to their tell-all answer to his trademark question: Would you let your mother/father drive your children on a mountain road?

Those who would reply in the negative sometimes notify the authorities about their fears, Locher says, but most older-driver referrals to the DMV come from law-enforcement officers and doctors. Health and safety codes in states like California mandate that physicians report patients with any condition that may impair driving.

"That's pretty vague," Iverson says. "If you want to follow the letter of the law, which stipulates 'the loss of ability to perform a single activity of daily living,' then having trouble brushing teeth because of a tremor is a reportable condition."

Such a report is intended to trigger a re-examination of the driver, but Iverson worries that the current fiscal crisis plaguing so many state governments may push officials to revoke the license summarily, without any costly testing.

Undaunted by the extra expense such a proposal might require, some favor national screening standards for keeping mature drivers safely on the road.

"Just as there are age recommendations for beginning screening for prostate cancer and colon cancer, due to the increased incidence of these conditions with age, there should be more intensive screening of drivers who reach an age associated with elevated safety risks – in addition to evaluations of individuals diagnosed with dementia at any age," Wadley urges.

"On average, at age 65, the incidence of motor-vehicle collisions increases and, beginning at age 75, the likelihood of dying in a crash rises, due to frailty of the musculoskeletal system."

Others, like Locher, see any countrywide screening plans as unworkable.

"Driving in California is not the same as driving in Florida, Minnesota, Louisiana, Nevada, or any other state," he maintains. "Screening and additional testing should be done on a case-by-case basis, initiated by events or conditions, not age."

Locher opposes any driving tests – either simpler or more difficult than the routine ones – aimed solely at seniors.

"The only fair thing is to actively go after bad drivers and leave proven good drivers alone, regardless of age," he contends. "We do have an alternate [driving] test for those with certain medical conditions, but this … test is the same regardless of the age of the driver."

A complete cultural overhaul at the California DMV has shifted the agency's singular direction of testing and licensing toward the broader aim of keeping drivers on the road for as long as it is safe to do so, says Fenner, a 53-year veteran of the agency.

Among other changes, seniors who fail the driving test three times, but whose errors the examiner views as "reversible," may now get a fourth try before having their license revoked.

"Just as with teens starting out," Fenner says, "if you fail three times, we give you permission to drive with someone in the car while you study for the next test, and we may require a driving lesson or two. If you still can't pass the next test, then it's time to say, 'Charley, give up the keys.'"

That may be easier said than driven home.

"When confronted with the inevitable, the response is on a continuum, from agreement and acquiescence to total denial, anger and hostility," Iverson says. "The end of driving can be associated with worsening of depression and shortened life expectancy."

Little wonder, given the commonplace conviction that an end to driving is an end to life as we know it in America.

Yet, with proper preparation, planning, and positive outlook, it need not be.

5. The Daisy Decelerator

by Robert A. Comunale, M.D.

1829

"Rupert dear, have you seen this?"

"Yes, Abigail, I've already read the newspaper."

"Rupert, it says that Mr. Stephenson's steam engine, the Rocket, reached a speed of 24 miles per hour at the Liverpool and Manchester Railway. How can that be?"

"My dear, I'm sure it's just some folderol from those boys at the Times in London. After all, man wasn't meant to travel that fast. It would kill us."

"My goodness!"

Gentle Abigail probably would have fainted outright had she heard the velocities at which we humans travel today, nearly two centuries later, where cruising along an interstate at 65 miles per hour can draw horns, frowns and middle-digit gestures if the speed limit is 70.

Obviously, velocity won't kill us. Highway travel aside, people routinely cross the countryside at speeds above 100 mph on trains. They fly over nations and oceans comfortably at 500 mph or more in airliners. And they even orbit Earth 16 times a day at nearly 18,000 mph.

What can do us great harm is too-rapid acceleration or deceleration, particularly when our mode of transportation meets a point of impact.

Stopping Versus Slamming

At our age, none of us is likely to jump into a rocket sled and experience hazardous g-forces as we accelerate to maximum speed within a second or two. Only a handful of us still qualify to ride in high-performance jets or handle NHRA dragsters over a quarter-mile course.

No, acceleration is not a big concern for seniors – but deceleration is.

The problem is inertia, a concept formulated by Sir Isaac Newton in the late 17th century. Simply put, it means that a body either at rest or in motion will remain in that state indefinitely unless some outside force affects it. For our purposes it means that whenever you ride in a vehicle and that vehicle comes to a sudden stop, your body will continue to move forward unless it's restrained.

In other words, if your vehicle hits something, such as a vehicle stopped ahead of you or, worse, a vehicle moving in the opposite direction, the initial impact will stop your vehicle. But you will continue to move until you also hit something.

Half a century ago this was an enormous problem, because few vehicles were equipped with seat belts, let alone airbags, crumple zones, rigid passenger cages and related safety devices. Half a century ago, if your vehicle hit something hard enough, chances are your body wouldn't stop moving until it crashed through the windshield and onto the pavement. That's why, in the United States, we regularly suffered 50,000-plus highway deaths a year – the equivalent of over 100,000 deaths with today's population.

Because of this horrendous toll, scientists and automotive engineers began exploring ways of minimizing the root cause of the fatalities: sudden deceleration. They needed to find out just how much deceleration the human body could safely tolerate. So they built a device called the Daisy Decelerator. Essentially, it was a sled with rockets on the back and wheels to convey it down a set of rails where it ultimately hit a barricade.

Recipe: take one human, fit it into a pressure suit, place it on the Daisy (named for the famous air rifle), fire the rockets and see what happens.

What happened was the tearing of muscles and ligaments all over the body and the fracture of bones.

When Metal Meets Metal

Based on tests endured by brave volunteers who rode the Daisy sled – along with the modern crash-test dummies used today – we know quite a bit about what affects your body during a collision. It depends on four critical factors: the speed of the two colliding vehicles, the direction and placement of the impact, the safety systems of your vehicle, and whether you're strapped properly into your seat belt.

These factors combine to establish the outcome in less time than you can snap you fingers twice.

Here, basically, is what happens:

Your front bumper slams into the other vehicle's front bumper – not head-on but sort of halfway, covering only the driver's side of each vehicle. This is how most frontal crashes occur that involve two vehicles of approximately equal size. The combined forces of the impact push the portion of the bumper and grill receiving the collision about two feet into the engine compartment. The impact also crushes the front lights, buckles the hood, bulges the fenders outward, and causes vehicle fragments to fly off in all directions. To an outsider the front ends of both vehicles look like they're exploding.

Somewhere under that contorting hood, with lightening speed, a sensor determines that the airbags are needed. It sends a signal to the two control units –one inside the steering wheel, the other on the passenger side of the dashboard.

Nearly instantaneously those two units inflate the airbags – in reality they detonate them, at the speed of a Major League Baseball player's swing, sending them screaming out of their containers.

Just in time, too. Like a pizza shoved off a platter into an oven you slide forward in the seat as your vehicle comes to a stop. The airbag smacks your face hard, like a boxer hitting a punching bag, but it slows your momentum just as the seat belts grab hold of you with ferocity. Your head, arms and legs all snap forward.

The strain on your muscles, spine and joints is severe. For an instant your eyeballs each weigh 10 pounds. It's fortunate that by reflex your eyelids have clamped shut tightly. Otherwise your eyes might shoot out of your skull.

Your legs absorb a powerful shock as the floor panel buckles and kicks back at them. That shock, plus the resistance of the airbag and seat belts, shoves your body backward toward the seat. At the same time the "offset" force of the crash whips the rear end of the vehicle sideways toward the passenger side, while you slip in the opposite direction toward the door. If you're lucky, or if your vehicle is equipped with side-impact airbags, you avoid hitting your head.

A few seconds after the impact – it might have seemed like hours to you because your perception of time seems to slow way down – both you and your vehicle come to a complete stop. By then the vehicle's front end is a mangled mess. The radiator has burst, spewing scalding antifreeze and steam. The battery may have exploded. The hood is bent upward like a metal pup tent. The engine block has been knocked off its mountings. The windshield is shattered. A mixture of fluids drains onto the roadway.

Much more important is the possible damage to you. It may include cuts and bruises on your face, hands, shoulders, abdomen and legs – anywhere your body came in contact with the airbag, seat belt, steering wheel or other parts of the vehicle's interior. Your nose may have been broken; likewise bones in your feet, ankles or shins, depending on the severity of the shock from the floor panel. And if you've hit the side door with your head, you may have suffered a concussion.

Chances are, though, you're still alive. The reason: Your collision occurred at 40 miles per hour, the approximate upper limit of safety in all of today's vehicles.

It's hard to believe, but as violent and chaotic as the collision may have seemed, much of your vehicle's behavior was by design, the product of decades of painstaking automotive-safety research and engineering – the combined efforts of people in the manufacturing companies, the highway safety community, federal and state governments, and the insurance industry.

Natural Defenses

The healthy human body boasts several effective means of protecting itself from damaging critical organs during the sudden deceleration of a collision:

The skin acts like a plastic bag to hold in the body's contents.

The bony skeleton provides attachment points for muscles, a vault for the brain, and a cage for the heart and lungs.

The muscles can tense to hold our softer tissues in place.

The ligaments act as restraints of last resort to keep everything else from flying apart.

Now, let's talk about aging. All those protective elements change as our bodies
get older:

We naturally lose water, fat and structural minerals.

Our bones become more brittle, even if we fight the process by taking calcium, vitamin D and bisphosphonates to help reverse bone thinning.

The padding of fat under the skin thins out, even in big folks.

The elastic component of the skin diminishes so it tears instead of flexing.

The brain, sitting in a fluid-filled, triple-layered sack, starts to shrink.

The Limits of Safety

To put it another way, old Mother Nature isn't nice when it comes to aging and trauma, no matter how well engineered our vehicles are. Consider this scenario, built with fictional characters but using physical and physiological fact:

Ilsa Seligman was one happy lady.

It was her 89th birthday. She was about to be taken to Sunday brunch by her lovely granddaughter and her two adorable great-grand-children. Dressed to go in her blazer, skirt and cashmere sweater, she glanced at the hallway mirror, wistfully admiring the remnants of youthful beauty on her face. She wished her Ira was still with her. She had lost him six months ago but it still seemed like yesterday.

"Come on, Grandma, we're ready to leave."

She smiled in recognition. How many times had she called and herded her children out the front door. Now her granddaughter Miriam, the mother of two youngsters, echoed that admonition.

Ilsa moved slowly. Her eyesight and hearing were not what they used to be, either. But she made it out the front door, without difficulty and on her own, then down the porch steps and sidewalk toward the family car.

She saw Miriam securing Rachel, her two-year-old great-grand-daughter, in the child-safety seat. Her great-grandson Jacob, age three and already secured, wiggled and squirmed at the restraints.

"Meemaw, can you sit back here with me?"

Rachel was the only one who called her that.

"No, dear, I need to sit up front with your mom."

She still missed her daughter Judith, a victim of breast cancer a decade earlier. But Miriam helped to fill that sad, sad loss.

Ilsa climbed into the front seat and fumbled with the shoulder belt. Miriam helped her click it into place, started the engine, and slowly moved out the driveway and down the street toward the town center and the nice family restaurant they both liked so much.

A few blocks later the traffic light ahead turned red.

Miriam slowed and stopped the car. The driver behind them, pre-occupied on a cell-phone call, did not. She failed to stop in time and crunched into their back bumper. The seat belts and head restraints did their jobs and held the two adults and two toddlers in place.

"Great! Just what I need today," Miriam fumed.

She felt the tightness in her neck. The low-speed impact from

behind had caused a classic head-bobble reaction that had sent her
neck muscles into a spasm.

She looked in the rearview mirror at the children. They looked a
little distressed but otherwise fine. Then she turned to Ilsa.

"You okay, Grandma?"

"Grandma? Grandma!"

We have made great progress in protecting child passengers in our vehicles. Warnings, laws, improved safety and booster seats all have resulted in steady declines in injuries and deaths.

But we're not applying the same effort to protecting our elderly. Our safety priorities are not keeping up with demographics.

As Dr. Williams pointed out earlier, the U.S. senior population – including senior drivers – is booming. We're living longer and remaining active at ages that rendered our ancestors either disabled or deceased.

Part of that activity involves highway travel, and the more we drive or ride on the roads, the greater our chances of becoming involved in one of the 20,000 or so collisions that occur every day. We face that risk with "equipment" that has suffered quite a bit of wear and tear.

For those lucky enough to survive into their 80s and beyond, life has taken a toll on their bodies. In particular, the human skeleton, the infrastructure that keeps us upright, weakens significantly in seniors. Osteoporosis of the spine and hips can begin as early as the fourth decade of life.

By the sixth decade, almost everyone, male or female, shows some thinning in crucial weight-bearing areas like the upper thighs and hip joint. The discs that separate the vertebrae become more viscous – less flexible – drying out and shrinking to the point where bone can press against bone and irritate nerve roots that extend out from in between.

It's inevitable, and no amount of exercise, extra calcium, vitamin D and drugs that are supposed to reverse osteoporosis can completely overcome it. Likewise, genetics, body build, gender and ethnicity all eventually succumb.

By the time individuals reach their 80s, they've become highly susceptible to shear forces and what's known as the bobble effect – aka coup contrecoup – of auto crashes. Likewise, arthritic changes and bone thinning can cause a part of the second cervical vertebra – aka the axis – to snap off and cause fatal damage to the brain and spinal cord.

In fact, any vertebra can shift and cause spinal-cord damage that wouldn't normally happen in a younger person.

A Litany of Decline

Another body component that shows wear and tear with age is the vascular system – the blood vessels – which can develop weaknesses not easily manifest until an individual is subjected to blunt trauma.

For example, the aorta, the major artery of the heart, accumulates weakness in one or all of its three layers: the tunica adventitia or outer layer, the heavily muscular tunica media or middle layer, and the tunica intima or inner layer. When that elastic tissue weakens, the result is an aneurysm, a balloon-like condition that can rupture very suddenly.

Then there's the brain, sitting in its fluid-filled sack within the skull. Time shrinks brain tissue, so there's more and more space between the brain and the inner skull. When a person experiences an impact, such as sitting in an automobile that hits or is struck by something, the effect is a bobble of the head. The brain, like the rest of the body, had been traveling along with the vehicle. An impact causes the vehicle to stop abruptly, but the brain keeps on moving, banging into the inside front of the skull and then bobbing backward against the back side.

This can occur several times – the aforementioned coup contrecoup injury –tearing blood vessels in the process and causing bleeding inside and around the brain.

As for the vascular system, seat belts may save lives, but they can also kill people.

Let me repeat: Seat belts can kill.

Airbags aren't the only potentially lethal devices inside our vehicles.

The compression force of a tensioned seat belt on the chest wall can cause bruising of the heart and, particularly in the elderly, massive rib fractures that can penetrate the heart as surely as a bullet.

Even if the ribs remain intact, if the vascular system is harboring an aneurysm, a sudden compression from impact with a seat belt can create a massive hemorrhage that can kill within seconds.

Maybe it's time for our automotive engineers to design additional padding and energy-absorbing frames in vehicles, particularly those favored by seniors.

The emergency medical tech touched Ilsa Seligman's motionless forehead and pulled back her eyelids. Her right pupil was fixed and dilated, staring into eternity.

He shook his head.

"Brain hemorrhage."

6. Our Driving Brethren Aren't Helping
by Phil Berardelli

Though it will be some time before I become one, I have given in-depth thought to senior drivers, many of whom live in my neighborhood. I've noticed that many of them [drive] really slow, which can be as unsafe as driving too fast and which, I'll admit, annoys me.

– Joe H., 22

As Dr. Comunale explained, both our driving skills and physical resilience – our personal crashworthiness – decline as we age. Not that we were so safe on the roads when we were younger. Driving is and for the last six decades has been the most dangerous thing we all do every day, to the point that if we're going to die from accidental causes there's a fairly high probability it's going to be in an automobile, most likely within a few miles of home.

Sure, many health risks increase as we age – heart disease, cancer, stroke, diabetes, osteoporosis, to name a few. But highway crashes represent an ever-present danger that spans our lives, with effects every bit as sudden, violent and tragic as deaths in wartime, and they don't recede just because we don't drive as far or fast, or in bad weather or at night.

Along with watching our weight and diet, re-assessing our driving skills is a smart way to improve the odds of enjoying our Golden Years to the fullest.

Assessing the Risk
Let's start by taking a look at what we're facing.

A terrible carnage pervades our streets, roads and highways, and it isn't the work of terrorists, criminals or lunatics run amok.

It's being caused by ordinary, usually well-intentioned people who become impaired with alcohol or drugs; who disobey speed limits, stop signs, traffic lights and lane markers, and who routinely ignore other rules of the road, not to mention the basics of common courtesy.

How much carnage? In terms of death we lose about 33,000 souls annually at current rates, with injuries running around 3 million per year. True, those are big drops from where the figure was just a few years ago, and even bigger reductions from the horrible annual tolls seen in the 1950s and early '60s – among a much-smaller driving population. Still, they remain unacceptably high numbers.

Think a Vietnam War's worth of losses in less than two years, or an Iraq War every couple of months – or a 9/11 every six weeks.

That's what ordinary drivers are doing to one another.

Yes, men and women of all ages, ethnic stripes, religious denominations, community organizations and occupations are contributing to the careless, frenetic and downright dangerous environment on our highways, an environment that becomes increasingly difficult to handle as our faculties begin to diminish.

Even if you've never been involved in a crash yourself it's a near certainty you've encountered a bad one or its aftermath.

I often speak to groups of parents in connection with my book *Safe Young Drivers: A Guide for Parents and Teens*. When I do I talk about the culture of our highways. It's significantly different from the times when humans populated small communities or villages, where the elders tended to guide youngsters along the path to adulthood, where everyone knew and looked out for one another.

Translated into the transportation milieu it means motorists grant no patience or courtesy to young and inexperienced drivers. They give youngsters no more room than anyone else. They tailgate them and refuse to forgive their faults as much as anyone else.

It's even more so with people of advancing age. As we naturally and reflexively take longer to make driving moves, particularly in heavy traffic, we begin to draw negative attention from our fellow motorists. Wait an extra few seconds to pull out onto a highway, or to start out when the traffic light turns green, and we're liable to hear the assertive blast of a horn behind us.

So much for respect for elders. The older we get the more of a nuisance we seem to become. Instead of receiving patience and deference we're the subject of taunts, rudeness and ridicule. Comedians and late-night television hosts exploit our growing tentativeness for laughs. We enter the worst possible category for today's drivers: We're impediments to them getting to where they want to go as fast as they can.

'The Fury'

In a sense this makes us seniors the bookend equivalent of teens, with the youthful group representing inexperience, ours adopting wise discretion and extra caution, and both requiring extra-special care to handle the threat created by neighbors and fellow motorists.

Here's an example of what I'm talking about.

I live in the suburbs of Northern Virginia, outside Washington, D.C., a metropolitan area choked by some of the most massive traffic in the country. My home is located about a half-mile from a village center featuring shops, restaurants, a couple of supermarkets and various business establishments. As often as I can I walk into that commercial district, partly for exercise and partly to escape the effort required to find a convenient parking space. Every time I do this I witness the same thing.

The street where I walk contains a series of traffic signals, the first of them on the corner of my townhouse community. The volume is heavy most of the day but particularly so during the morning and evening rush hours and at lunchtime. During those intervals several dozen vehicles can be sitting at the intersection waiting for the light to change. When it does you'd think a NASCAR starter has dropped the green flag. Drivers gun their accelerators and take off, beginning a collective jockeying for position. They pass, weave back and forth between the lanes, and maybe even compete a little with nearby rivals.

Until…

That's right – until they all get to the next red light a couple of hundred yards down the strip. Then everyone stops, waits for the light to change, and starts the whole thing up again.

From inside of one of the vehicles things might seem unremarkable. But to someone on foot, watching it all unfold and seeing the result, it's rather obnoxious. I call it "the Fury," because it reminds me of that passage from Shakespeare's *Macbeth*:

Life's but a walking shadow, a poor player
That struts and frets his hour upon the stage
And then is heard no more: it is a tale
Told by an idiot, full of sound and fury,
Signifying nothing.
    – Act 5, Scene 5

When I first published *The Driving Challenge: Dare to Be Safer and Happier on the Road* over a decade ago, I attempted to focus attention on the vast amount of harm being caused on the highways by aggressiveness and bad manners. Now, with this book, and with the help of my colleagues, I'm continuing that effort, concentrating on a specific segment of the driving population, one less responsible for the harm but now more susceptible to its consequences.

We must face the facts that:

The chaotic environment of the roads will not change.

Our fellow motorists will offer us little consideration.

Our driving abilities will inevitably weaken.

Given these "challenges" we have no choice but to keep our guard up as effectively as possible for as long as possible.

7. Flavors of Aggression

by Phil Berardelli

I drive kinda recklessly, I take a lot of chances, I never repair my vehicles, and I don't believe in traffic laws.

– George Carlin

Outrageous comments aside, such as that one by the late Mr. Carlin, one of my favorite comedians, the greatest danger to everyone on the highways is caused by what Dr. Williams calls "everyday aggression," something many people practice routinely. It involves a frequent disregard for traffic laws and reasonable standards of courtesy.

It begins with speeding. Most drivers speed – up to 90 percent based on my direct, nearly daily observations for over a decade. They do it even though speeding, both exceeding posted speed limits and driving too fast for conditions, is one of the three most common causes of crashes. Another is driving while impaired; the third – and fastest growing – is distraction.

Speeding automatically endangers everyone in or around the offending vehicle. It is a form of aggressive driving. Even more than that, it has become a universal bad habit.

I'm not talking only about the expressways. Speeding is just as pervasive in neighborhoods. That's an important point for all drivers, especially for seniors, because speeders are hazardous to anyone needing to pull out of a driveway, a side street or a parking space, particularly when the view of oncoming traffic is obstructed.

Likewise, speeders cross paths with pedestrians, children, cyclists and animals.

In all such situations the ability to stop or slow down quickly is crucial.

Nevertheless many drivers refuse to slow down no matter what the conditions are. As a result motorists face a dangerous disadvantage anytime they try to pull onto a road – particularly one with limited visibility. They simply can't count on traffic moving slowly or carefully enough to permit a safe entrance. The same goes for pedestrians, particularly if they try to cross streets or roads away from designated crosswalks. And the most vulnerable of all, whether behind the wheel or on foot, are seniors.

Hair Triggers

It would be one thing if speeders were just being a little careless and anytime somebody or some situation reminded them of their lawlessness they'd immediately apologize, slow down and shape up.

Not likely. Many of these people carry negative emotions behind the wheel along with their propensity to drive too fast. Impatience, frustration, rudeness, anger and even the simmering tendency to want to intimidate or harm can inhabit their psyches. This particular example took place on a Russian highway but it reflects the emotions American drivers often display.

On-the-road behavior is different from person-to-person encounters on foot.

There, if you step in front of someone inadvertently and excuse yourself, chances are you'll receive a polite dispensation and not a second thought about it. But pull out suddenly in front of someone on the highway and it can be quite a different story. The same if you change lanes in too close proximity to another driver. True, safety is involved, but rudeness can arise even if you're in a crowded parking lot or trapped inside a traffic jam. People will throw tantrums if they can't move 10 feet or lose one place in a line of vehicles.

I recall two incidents. One happened on the Fourth of July after the annual fireworks display on the National Mall. As the display ended, and members of the peaceable crowd slowly dispersed and headed toward the city's Metro system and their vehicles, I saw a man in an SUV nearly run over a woman pushing a baby carriage –

just so he could move about 50 feet to become stuck in the huge post-event traffic jam.

The other occurred in downtown Manhattan in New York City. I was stopped at an intersection, even though the light was green, because there was no room on the other side. Suddenly the driver behind me began laying on his horn and angrily gesturing me to move ahead. When I didn't budge he swung around me and into the intersection ... only to get stuck there for several minutes, as cross traffic struggled to get around him.

I could describe many more incidents because it happens all the time. Years ago my local newspaper reported that a woman — six months pregnant – had bumped the vehicle of a former U.S. congressman. He got out, approached the woman, and punched her in the face so hard that he shattered her sunglasses and gave her a black eye.

Motorists often abandon all civility when they feel confined. An example occurred early one April morning in the late 1990s, when a vehicle overturned in a crash on an expressway in the Virginia suburbs, just south of Washington, D.C. The incident brought rush-hour traffic to a halt and caused a 15-mile backup.

One of the vehicle occupants, a young woman, had been thrown onto the pavement and lay there, injured. A nearby motorist rushed to her aid. As reported in The Washington Post, while the motorist, an Army major stationed at the Pentagon, waited for an ambulance to arrive, other vehicles attempted to push by the crash site, some of them moving dangerously close to the victim. Several drivers actually gestured and yelled angrily at the man, whose only crime was trying to keep the woman from being injured further.

It's not exactly a new phenomenon. Nasty-tempered drivers have been around as long as there have been highways. Violent confrontations have been reported for years. The Wall Street Journal ran a story on October 20, 1978, titled "Highway Massacre: Nowadays Carnage isn't all Accidental. Guns, Knives, Fists, and Cars Become Drivers' Weapons."

These days just about everyone involved with highway-safety

issues is alarmed, not so much about the extreme cases, which remain relatively rare, but about the widespread atmosphere of rudeness, selfishness and recklessness.

It crosses just about all demographic lines, from the most typical aggressive drivers – males between 18 and 35 – to individuals in other age ranges who would find such behavior offensive anywhere else, people who wouldn't think of being impolite off the road are routinely rude and impatient behind the wheel.

A careful, polite driving society would mitigate the risks for its eldest members. Lacking such an environment, it's imperative that we do everything we can on our own to reduce those risks.

PART II
Never Too Late to Drive Smarter

8. Return to the Basics
by Phil Berardelli

I like driving myself to the store at my convenience. I don't like having to rely on others.

– Lorraine H., 70

Old habits die hard. If you're approaching or already enjoying retirement you've probably spent half a century on the road and logged half-a-million miles or more.

Congratulations! That's quite an achievement – something unprecedented in human history. But you may have gotten here on cruise control. That is, except for those high school classes you took so long ago, you likely haven't given much thought to your driving techniques. You might still be performing behind the wheel the way you did at the beginning – except that your vision, hearing and reflexes are slowly but inexorably deteriorating.

That's why I'm going to concentrate on defensive techniques – effective ways to protect yourself from your younger and too-often aggressive fellow motorists.

As Dr. Williams pointed out in the first chapter, we seniors generally represent the safest highway demographic, particularly so when we're acting as grandparents transporting our grandkids. [57]

Furthermore, it's possible to maintain that safe reputation for years by meeting those inevitable changes in our physical performance head-on. We can't ignore them. For the rest of our lives, when it comes to driving, our best method of preparation is to assess our skills and habits periodically.

Call it just another facet of your continuing education. After all, you're probably diving eagerly into art and literature and history and dancing and cooking classes.

So how about taking some time, informally and at your convenience, to examine your skills as a driver? It can't hurt and you'll be glad you did.

The Checklist

Let's start with three vital concepts that are basic to keeping yourself and the others around you as safe as possible on the road:

Do you buckle your seat belt every time you get in the vehicle?

Do you make sure everyone else in your vehicle is belted – with babies and young children strapped properly into safety seats?

Do you ever drink or take drugs – including certain prescription medications – and drive?

These items probably should go without saying; likewise any suggestions about properly adjusting your mirrors and your seat to maximize comfort and visibility and maintaining a safe distance from the airbag in your steering wheel.

Probably, but some members of our driving demographic have never abided by the basics. If you're one of them here's a chance to refresh your competency at what has been a major life activity. As the chapter title suggests, as long as you're still driving it isn't too late to tone up.

Safe Driving Ground Zero

Let's move on to an item that may be a little less obvious but no less vital:

Slow down.

Change the familiar reading of your speedometer. Begin to use the most important safety device in your vehicle, the one that can produce the most immediate results in nearly every situation you're likely to encounter – your own right foot.

Ease up on it and slow down.

Yes, I know; seniors are often stereotyped as poking along, leading long lines of increasingly impatient drivers. Also, seniors tend to speed less than the general driving population. And, yes, some of our most senior drivers indeed do poke along. But that isn't what I'm talking about.

I mean using your speed as an effective defensive-driving strategy. The way to begin is to slow down – in a calculated way, both as a matter of course in normal driving conditions and even more when you need to stretch out your margin of safety.

How much? It depends on the situation, but three rules can help you:

+ Slow down to obey all speed limits.
+ Slow down relative to the traffic around you.
+ Slow down in response to changing conditions.

Topsy-Turvy

When I speak to groups about driving safety I often ask:

"What's a speed limit?"

I usually get something similar to these two answers:

"It's the maximum safe speed."

"It's the legal limit in good weather."

Then I give my own answer, which always elicits initial stunned looks followed by smiles and nods of recognition:

Yes, speed limits are set by highway engineers, who try to determine a safe and reasonable maximum speed for baseline road conditions – the estimated normal traffic load and driver skills on a clear day on dry pavement.

But, no, that isn't what I meant.

Just about everywhere in America the posted speed limits – whether on highways, streets or roads – have become minimum speeds.

Think about it. In today's driving environment it's a genuine rarity for a vehicle to be moving along at less than the maximum posted speed, especially when just about everybody else is going even faster. The formal definition is technically correct, but the informal one is what's true:

The maximum posted speed *is* the minimum consensual speed.

Combating Mass Mindlessness

Whatever the reasons – habit, ignorance, a genuine need to hurry – most of our fellow motorists are driving faster than is safe no matter where they're headed. I often hear people talking routinely about doing 5 miles an hour over the limit as if it were a meaningless distinction.

It's the civilian equivalent of mission creep.

Even the police aren't helping. Many officers won't write a ticket unless a motorist is doing at least 10 miles an hour over the limit; then they'll give you a break by designating the speed as 9 miles over, to keep you from getting hit with a more serious penalty.

Don't get me wrong; I'm not suggesting that cops should start citing people for going 56 miles per hour in a 55 zone. What I am saying is this attitude, as well as the unbridled competitive instinct of many drivers, has caused a dangerous uptick in the average speed of traffic, to the point where it is well above the legal limit for the vast majority of vehicles on any given roadway.

People even ignore the speed limits in their own neighborhoods.

For seniors, all this speeding intensifies the risk of being on the road because it cuts into our declining reaction times.

'Clear the Way'

I use this phrase to teach teenagers the basics but it works for any age or level of driving proficiency. I'll come back to it later; for now I want to mention it to address a major factor in avoiding collisions: stopping distance.

Take a vehicle going 65 miles an hour, an ordinary speed on most interstates nowadays. That translates into 95 feet per second – nearly a football field every three seconds.

Today's vehicles – whether or not they're equipped with antilock brakes or the other safety features John Matras describes in an upcoming chapter – take at least 3 seconds to stop completely. That interval includes the time for the average driver to spot a hazard, react to it by switching from the gas pedal to the brake, stomp on the brake pedal, and have the brakes halt the wheels from rolling – assuming everything in the sequence works perfectly.

Three seconds. At 65 miles an hour your stopping distance is around 285 feet – about 16 car lengths. On the open road, with good visibility and light traffic, distances greater than 285 feet are commonly available. In congested environments, however, that's rarely the case. Instead it's routine to see packs of vehicles going faster than 65 and separated by only a couple of car lengths.

The older you get the more safety margin you need.

How much?

If you're age 65 or older I recommend 3.5 seconds.

If you're 75 or older you should bump it to 4 seconds.

And if you're 85 or older your margin should be at least 5 seconds.

Useful Tip:
How do you gauge, say, 4 seconds while moving along a roadway? Easy. First check your speed. Then pick an object near the side of the road such as a utility pole. The instant you pass it begin counting: "One thousand one, one thousand two, one thousand three…" Just as you complete "one thousand four" check your rearview mirror to see how far you've traveled. That's your margin of safety at that speed.

Calculating the other timeframes works the same way. You can use this method no matter your speed because you're measuring distance traveled over time.

If you regularly practice it you'll begin to perceive automatically how much of a safety margin you need – something I call a clear zone.

What's the best way to maintain it?

Slow down.

It's simple. If you slow down you increase your clear zone; if you speed up you decrease it. At highway speeds, for seniors, if it's less than the recommended margin you're counting on the precise and predictable actions of everyone else nearby, the lack of hazards appearing suddenly, and the continued proper mechanical performance of your vehicle. Failing all that, your safety rests on your ability to react.

It's a losing proposition. Sooner or later in those circumstances you're going to goof. Either you or someone near you will fail to overcome the miscue. Then, bam! It's too late for the wisdom of hindsight.

Excessive speed is a leading cause of crashes for precisely that reason: too many vehicles going too fast in rapidly changing and unpredictable situations. It's an unfortunate and dangerous misperception on the part of many drivers that they possess the skills to keep them out of trouble. They don't.

It gets worse as we age.

The problem is like gaining weight. Because most of us look at ourselves in the mirror every day we don't see much change. But when friends or family members encounter us after a hiatus they can spot the extra pounds right away.

Subtle but important changes can occur behind the wheel as we age – such as an increase in reaction time. We think we can handle situations because maybe we've done so in the past. It would be terrible if we're wrong.

One of the best, plainly human descriptions of this phenomenon I've ever heard was from champion boxer Sugar Ray Leonard. Late in his career Leonard lost a stunner of a match to a lowly rated foe. Afterward a reporter asked him what happened. He explained that he knew in his mind exactly how to handle his opponent – but his body couldn't react in time.

From now on never forget Ray Leonard's humbling assessment of his diminished skills – it's happening to all of us.

Slow down.

I can guess what you're thinking: "You want me to be run off the road? Other drivers will be screaming at me, calling me unprintable names. I'll become just another stereotypical senior, poking along and holding things up."

No, you won't. That's a myth about highway traffic. I drive this way all the time – been doing so for nearly two decades. As long as I stay in the right lane no one ever bothers me. Sure, if you block the passing lane you'll bring out the worst in others. So stay in the right lane. Then people will ignore you. Furthermore you'll achieve two important goals:

You'll continually allow yourself a bigger safety margin.

You'll avoid the mindless tendency to keep up with traffic.

Mindless? Unfortunately yes. How many times have you read or heard in the news about huge pileups on fogbound highways or icy interstates, or that terrible crash on I-75 in Florida in late January 2012? [58]

Such disasters are caused because drivers bunch up too closely at unwise speeds. Then it takes only a small mistake by one member of the pack to cascade into something big and awful.

The Benefit of Easing Up

The one thing you don't want to do, however, is drive much slower than the speed limit in a traffic situation. That can be as dangerous as speeding, for different reasons.

The key to traffic safety is a smooth and consistent flow, which means everyone should be moving at approximately the same speed. The danger level quickly rises if there's a large variation. That's why many expressways also have a posted minimum speed limit – usually 40. You don't want to be in a situation where some vehicles are going more than 20 miles an hour faster – or slower – than others in close proximity.

"Wait a minute," you say. "On the one hand you want me to back off from traffic. On the other you're saying it's safer when everyone is going the same speed. Aren't you being inconsistent?"

Not at all. I said it's safer when everyone goes approximately the same speed. There's a difference. Speeds already vary within traffic, sometimes by large amounts, because some drivers push much faster than the posted limit. That's a main reason why our highways are so dangerous. The environment is one of competition;

just about everyone is trying to push ahead of everyone else. The pack instinct is powerful.

What I'm suggesting is a strategy that allows you to operate safely amid the packs – and it's simple: Hang back just a little. Ease your speed until you're going slightly slower than the traffic around you. It's a small enough change, relative to usual traffic flow, that it will make you safer without interfering with everyone else.

This strategy has two additional benefits. First, it will subtly encourage other drivers to follow suit. Instead of helping to perpetrate a dangerous condition you can create a little island of safety around you. Don't scoff at the idea; it's more effective than you think.

Second, there are open zones between the traffic packs.

Yes, that's right. I discovered this phenomenon, which I call traffic oases, quite inadvertently.

A long time ago I had to take a trip on a couple of very busy interstates in a car that wasn't mechanically up to par. I decided not to push my luck with it so I stayed in the right lane and set the cruise control at 55, the speed limit at the time.

Everyone else around me was doing 60 or more.

Within a very short time the traffic left me behind. I discovered my first oasis and suddenly I was driving alone.

Alone!

The pack I had been part of contained maybe 50 vehicles. A while later another pack of similar size approached. It swarmed around me and likewise left me behind. The pattern continued for the rest of the trip. Hundreds and hundreds of vehicles passed me over the course of my 5-hour drive.

Hard to believe but no one gave me as much as a sideways glance. Drivers who move in packs are used to passing other vehicles. Someone who's going a little slower than normal – and who stays in the right lane – receives little or no notice.

I, on the other hand, passed only a dozen vehicles, mostly trucks climbing hills, and they soon passed me again. As I keep saying, such is the way speed limits are regarded. But, ah, those oases! They were great. Each time I entered one I had the whole road to myself. No tension, no crowding – just me, my clunker and the beautiful rolling countryside.

For the first time in my driving life I actually discovered peace on an interstate. I felt truly happy.

In the years since, I've taken trips to many destinations – driving much better wheels. If I stick to the plan the oases appear every time. They are the rule not the exception.

Oases exist on urban highways, too. Sometimes, even during rush hour, an empty pocket will appear to my continuing amusement. If you slow down to the speed limit or relative to traffic you will discover oases as well.

You might ask: "Why not just slip into an oasis then speed up to stay between two packs?"

Unfortunately you can't because oases are transitory spaces. They are temporary, appearing and disappearing, disintegrating and reforming, as the most aggressive drivers break out from the front of packs only to bunch up at the back of others. If you try to stay at the back of one pack you'll soon be engulfed by the leaders of the next one. It's unavoidable.

Better to proceed at a moderate speed and let the packs flow around you. Enjoy the oases as they appear, each one a temporary island refuge in the great sea of frenetic American highway traffic.

One caution: My longtime observations have revealed that the most aggressive drivers tend to bunch up at the back of the packs. Why? I'm not sure, but I suspect it's related to human psychology. If you're stuck behind a group of vehicles your natural tendency is to want to push through them, which increases your aggressive tendencies.

Get to the front of the pack, however, and that pushing urge subsidies. You tend to ease up a little. Then, instead of feeling frustrated by the vehicles ahead of you, your irritation switches to the vehicles behind you trying to get past.

Citing George Carlin again, no one has ever encapsulated this phenomenon better:

Have you ever noticed when you're driving that anyone who's driving slower than you is an idiot, and anyone driving faster than you is a maniac?

Learn to Drive 'Backwards'

Here's another way to think about easing up: Drive "backwards."

Excuse me?

Obviously I'm not being literal. What I am recommending, as a reliable defensive tactic, is that on multilane roadways you always move a little slower than the traffic around you. If you do you'll create the illusion that you're backing away from those vehicles.

It's a variation of Einstein's Theory of Relativity, which states that in space-time there's no single, objective viewpoint. Einstein explained that two observers, one riding a train passing a station, and the other standing on the station platform, would view the experience in two, equally valid ways. The person on the stationary platform would watch the train come roaring by, while the passenger on the train would see the station appearing to pass by. (We won't get into whether the train should have stopped at the station.)

If you practice driving backwards regularly you'll feel more confident about your ability to handle what's happening ahead of you on the road. The traffic around you will always seem to be plunging forward while you're hanging back cautiously and observing the developing scene – and able to stop safely if need be.

It's an altogether positive experience.

Back away – gently. You'll be amazed at how quickly you'll feel comfortable doing it – and uncomfortable if you resume keeping up with the pack.

Watch Out for Clogs

Often on interstates or other highways an individual lane can become blocked while the adjoining lanes remain open. It can happen because of a crash, construction or an exit or merge lane that has become overloaded.

In such cases, where part of the traffic is either stopped or crawling along, you want to be extremely cautious about passing by it at normal speed. Serious crashes have occurred because drivers have collided with vehicles trying to jump out of clogged lanes.

Remember, it's dangerous anytime the speed of traffic varies widely on the same roadway. That can be the case even if only one vehicle is speeding while the rest of traffic is slowed or stopped. It's dangerous because so many drivers possess that instinctive urge to break free. Anytime a traffic clog forms, vehicles are going to be shifting lanes suddenly. The resulting chaos can end in tragedy.

Useful tip:
Anytime you're in an open lane, but traffic is crawling in the lane next to you, slow down until your speed is no more than 20 miles an hour faster than the speed of that lane. If traffic is stopped in the lane beside you, creep along at 20 for as long as the clog persists.

Two corollaries:

If you're two lanes away from stalled traffic, slow down to 30 miles an hour above the speed of that traffic.

If you're three lanes away, slow down to 40 miles an hour above the speed of that traffic.

I'm completely serious. If traffic next to you is stopped, you must drop your speed because it's highly likely that someone will try to jump from that lane to the open lane. I see it all the time – and I'll bet you do, too – and you don't want to be rolling up on that vehicle at the speed limit when it happens.

If this seems too radical or complicated an approach, if it's something you can't bring yourself to do, at least do this: Take your foot off the gas and be ready to stop until you pass by the clog. Then if someone makes a sudden move you can brake more quickly. Ease by the clog and resume speed on the other side. Exercise a few seconds of patience and avoid hours of inconvenience and perhaps years of remorse.

Two-Lane Byplay

Driving the speed limit on two-lane roads is different from doing it on four-lane roads and expressways. If you're going the speed limit you'll start collecting a crowd. That is, speeders will start bunching up behind you. Given the realities of the roads this is a certainty. You can start out on a completely empty route with no one in your rearview mirror. Very soon, however, someone will show up back there.

Then what do you do? Two things:

First, resist the urge to speed up. Stick to the limit. The law is on your side.

Second – and this is extremely important – don't do anything to impede another driver. Most people will stay behind a vehicle doing the speed limit with no problems and pass at the first legal opportunity.

Yes, there are the constantly aggressive motorists. They almost can't bear to feel bottled up behind someone else. They may try to intimidate you by tailgating, flashing their lights, or hitting their horn. They may also display aggression by revving their engine or weaving within the lane.

If any of this happens you must resist your own worst urges. You know, as everyone should, that nothing makes a driver angrier than feeling deliberately blocked by someone else. Some of the most horrifying episodes of road rage have been triggered by this type of behavior.

By all means don't make the situation worse. Maintain your speed then move to the right at the first opportunity to let the aggressor go by. If you feel endangered pull off the road entirely.

Such confrontations will be rare. They've only happened to me a few times. The worst was a truck driver who actually tried to pass me on the shoulder because I had slowed to obey a flashing school zone warning light.

Heaven knows what goes on in the minds of such people.

Closer to Home

Slowing down and obeying speed limits don't just apply to interstates. You need to be particularly aware of your speed in your own neighborhood – where statistically you're most likely to be involved in a crash.

Secondary roads and streets post lower speed limits for a reason: They contain more frequent hazards, and sometimes those "hazards" need to be protected from you.

Whenever you're driving along familiar territory you might feel comfortable cheating on the speed limit, zipping by side streets and driveways without a care.

Why? The key word is "familiar." Exploring an unknown neighborhood makes you naturally cautious and uncertain – you don't quite know what to expect. But driving around in an area where you've lived for years you know what's around the bend.

Or do you?

Approaching a blind curve, are you sure there's no one about to pull out of a driveway?

Tooling down your own cul-de-sac, how do you know if a couple of the neighbor's kids aren't about carry their game of tag suddenly into the street?

Just because you've driven a route 999 times doesn't mean it carries no hazards on the thousandth time. Try not to lull yourself into a false sense of security. If you can't see around a corner, or over the top of a rise, it could be just as dangerous in your own backyard as in an unfamiliar neighborhood.

Also, think about what it's like when you're the one trying to pull out. Isn't it nerve-wracking? Speeding vehicles don't give you as much time as you should have to complete a safe maneuver. Too often you have to watch nervously for an opening and pull out faster than you'd like to avoid being broadsided.

Many crashes occur because people waiting to pull out grow impatient and decide to make an ill-fated dash for it. Or they have difficulty keeping track of every vehicle approaching them – something we'll cover shortly.

That's why it's just as important for you to slow down at home as anywhere else.

Safety Even When You're Alone

The slow-down rules I've described above will help to make you safer in traffic. My next rule can make you safer even when you're the only one on the road:

Slow down in response to conditions.

You may not have thought of this before, but as important as steering is it's equally as important to adjust your speed. You have to accelerate when you start out. You have to position yourself in traffic. You have to slow for curves or possible hazards, to stop at intersections or your destination, and slow or stop to avoid bumping into things. You take all these actions in response to road conditions, not just speed limits.

Most drivers give very little thought to how fast they should go at a particular moment. That's why so many drivers become their own worst enemies. They either have no idea what their proper speed should be or they're dangerously overconfident about it.

Adjusting your speed precisely can pay big dividends in terms of safety. It involves training yourself to go only as fast as stopping safely will permit.

In other words, always match your speed to your clear zone.

Here's an example:

You're driving along a winding country road full of blind curves, hidden driveways, hill crests and intersections. If you follow the speed limit the whole time you'll frequently be putting yourself in danger of hitting something.

The same with city streets with their usual lines of parked vehicles, entrances, alleys and intersections controlled either by signals or stop signs. Again, if you go the speed limit the whole time you'll be overdriving your situation. That's because the speed limit is the maximum permitted on that stretch of pavement. It only applies on the straightaways, where and when you have plenty of room and visibility. The rest of the time you need to go more slowly, depending on two things:

+ How far you can see in front of you.

+ How close potential hazards are to you.

If you're doing, say, 35 along the road, that's about 50 feet per second, about as long as the average ranch-style house from our youth. Typical stopping distance at that speed is about 150 feet, so if you want to be safe at all times at 35 you should keep that much of a clear zone ahead of you.

That is why it has become so dangerous on secondary roads and neighborhood streets as well as in parking lots and garages. Such places are loaded with potential hazards: curves made blind by hedges or trees, hidden driveways, abrupt hilltops, lanes obscured by parked vehicles and so on. Anywhere such things exist your clear zone quickly disappears if you're driving at or above the speed limit.

Because you can't change the landscape, or the crowded conditions of a parking lot, the only responsible option you have in such situations is to slow down – whatever the speed limit. If you're doing 35, and you can only see 50 feet ahead of you because of a curve or a hilltop, you're vulnerable. If a vehicle suddenly pulls out of a driveway 55 feet ahead, or a child on a bicycle rides into the street, or a pet dog or cat tries to dash across the road, you're going to hit it because you won't be able to stop in time.

If your visibility drops to 50 feet – about three car lengths – your safe speed in that situation is no more than 20.

Trusting Yourself

I've just used quite a few numbers involving safe stopping distances. You might worry that you'll never be able to remember any of them. Don't. Forget the numbers. Your own senses of speed and distance can work instinctively for you, as long as you practice them regularly. What you will have to remember is that your speed must always be consistent with your ability to see ahead.

Slow down until you're sure you can stop safely in time no matter what happens in front of you.

Even if you've been driving the same way for decades, even if you've never thought this way before, you can still develop this ability. Just practice it. Begin to be aware of how far ahead you can see at any given moment and keep asking yourself whether you could stop within that distance if you had to.

Useful tip:
Anytime your ability to see the road ahead is blocked, even briefly, imagine that someone is standing in the middle of the lane just out of your sight. Then ask yourself if you could stop in time to avoid hitting that person. Keep using that "What if..." question because you never want to experience such a situation for real.

Adapt, Adapt

My just-mentioned slow-down rule has two variations. The first is that your clear zone can change with conditions even if your speed doesn't.

Take icy roads for example. Under the best possible reaction time it's going to take longer to stop on frozen pavement – sometimes twice as long – than on a dry road. In icy conditions you have two choices: Maintain a much bigger clear zone or cut your speed in half. The critical thing to remember is that you have to make at least one of these choices.

Another good example: You're driving in traffic and maintaining a proper clear zone but then another vehicle passes and slips in front of you. Suddenly you don't have enough room to stop safely. What do you do?

Slow down until your clear zone is restored.

The second variation is to slow down to protect anyone or any living thing that could be endangered by your vehicle.

Just like fastening seat belts and not driving drunk, this is something that should be obvious. Judging from what I've observed in the behavior of so many drivers, however, it isn't. They refuse to slow down for pedestrians, cyclists, school buses and even children playing near roadways. They ignore pets and wild animals roaming nearby. They zoom through highway construction zones and crash sites.

The consequence: Thousands of people are struck and killed by vehicles each year, hundreds of thousands are injured, and uncounted millions of animals suffer the same fate.

Some people argue that hitting an animal is preferable to causing a crash with another vehicle. Who says the situation has to be either/or? Usually what happens in such cases is someone reacted to an animal too late and slammed on the brakes, forcing emergency evasive action by the other driver.

If that person had started to slow down at the first sight of the animal, events would have proceeded at a more gradual pace. The key thing to remember is all animals act unpredictably – especially when confronted by large, unfamiliar objects that move quickly but in straight lines. The best way to deal with that unpredictability is to begin to slow down immediately.

By slow down I don't mean hit the brakes. Those bumper stickers that advise "Warning: I Brake for Animals" are conscientious but misguided. Whenever you see an animal take your foot off the gas immediately and keep it off until you pass.

Let yourself coast for a while. You'll be better prepared for a sudden move by the animal and you'll give drivers behind you more time to react.

Useful tip:
What about animals already in the road, such as cats, dogs or squirrels? Try tapping your horn a few times. Animals have a tough time dealing with vehicles but they all respond quickly and predictably to loud noises. Chances are they'll instinctively flee the sound of your horn.

To Review
Slow down.
   Obey all speed limits.

Stay in the right lane on expressways and four-lane streets and highways.

Slow down relative to the traffic around you.

Don't deliberately obstruct faster traffic on two-lane highways.

Slow down in response to changing conditions (or) slow down until your speed matches your clear zone.

This might seem difficult but it can be done. I practice all of these techniques daily. Now that I'm becoming a senior driver it's more important than ever that I do so.

I try to remind myself that I'm no longer able to handle emergency situations on the road as easily and rapidly as I did when I was younger – just as Sugar Ray Leonard found out at an advanced boxing age when he faced an inferior opponent in the ring.

Remember what happened to him.

9. For Us, Maybe Even More Important
by Phil Berardelli

I sometimes make all right turns to get where I need to go, rather than pulling into traffic and feeling unsafe. I also don't like getting trapped between two huge SUVs in a parking lot, so I'll often park farther away and walk a little more, just so I can get back out without worrying.

– Lorraine H., 70

Another rule of safe driving for seniors is just as essential as slowing down:

Look where you're going.

Too obvious? Possibly, but not to everyone. Failure to look where you're going is one of the three major causes of crashes for all ages, along with driving while impaired and driving too fast for conditions. The deficiency is receiving more attention lately under the term "distracted driving," especially when talking on cell phones or texting is concerned.

Americans are busy, with too much to do and not enough time. As a result tension and frustration rise behind the wheel. Aggression and excessive speed are common on the highways; so is distraction.

I've seen the dangers of even momentary inattention many times. Once, years ago, while riding with one of my daughters on a rainy day along an interstate, I was trying to figure out her unfamiliar and complicated car stereo panel. After I had fiddled with it unsuccessfully she impatiently reached over to correct me.

She took her eyes off the road for no more than a couple of seconds and I was still concentrating on the control panel. When we both looked back up we were horrified. She had drifted onto the paved shoulder and was closing fast on a car that had parked too near the highway. We both gasped as my daughter swerved in the nick of time to avoid a high-speed collision.

Likewise I've allowed myself to become momentarily distracted while driving. More often than I'd like to admit, I've regained my attention just in time to be startled by a near miss.

I've learned my lessons:

Never assume the road ahead is clear.

Always look where you're going.

Distractions aren't the only problem. Here are four examples of what can get you into trouble:

1. You pull up to a stop sign to make a right turn and look exclusively left for oncoming traffic, completely neglecting to look to the right to see what might be directly in front of your vehicle.

If so, for a few seconds you're heading in one direction while looking in the opposite direction. Heaven help anything or anyone who happens to cross your path. I've seen pedestrians nearly run over because they attempted to cross at a stop sign or traffic light in front of someone who was looking left but turning right.

If you're turning right of course you want to check to the left to see what's coming. But you also have to look ahead – to the right – before you move. Hazards can emerge from that direction, too. Along with pedestrians or joggers there could be a kid on a bike. There could even be a vehicle stopped just around the corner. If so, and if you continue to move without looking, you're going to hit what's there.

2. Entering a highway from a merge ramp you twist your head around to watch for traffic approaching from behind. While you do you're moving blindly into what's ahead. That's asking for trouble. If the merge lane is short – or, in the most dangerous case, if there's no merge area at all – you could easily run out of room or even run off the road because you haven't looked at what's directly in front of you.

Worse, if someone ahead is stopped on that ramp, you're headed for a collision.

Here's a variation: You stop at the end of an entrance ramp or merge lane even when there's plenty of room to keep going. You've focused your attention on the traffic behind you and forgotten to watch what's ahead.

Once I saw a vehicle stopped at the end of a ramp that actually was the beginning of a whole new lane. The driver, looking back at constant traffic, was waiting to merge even though nothing but empty pavement lay in front of him.

Anytime you're merging onto an expressway, ask:

Is the merge area missing or is there an open merge lane?

Is there a temporary acceleration lane or is it the start of an additional traffic lane?

Is traffic on the merge lane moving ahead of you or is it backed up?

The way you answer these questions is to focus first on what's ahead.

3. A common cause of crashes on crowded highways is changing lanes without clearing blind spots. These are zones to the side and back of your vehicle that you can't see in your mirrors. If you only look in your mirrors before turning or changing lanes – and some drivers don't even do that – and if there's another vehicle in one of your blind spots, you could easily smack into it or it could smack into you. The same goes if you're caught in a traffic clog and you try to jump to an adjacent lane without first making sure it's clear.

4. Another frequent source of collisions: You pull out of a side street, or pull out or back out of driveways or parking spaces, without looking. If you're entering a street or a road you need to continue looking for traffic until you've completed your turn. A quick glance won't do it, especially when so many other drivers speed, because someone could be upon you in a flash. Backing up requires even more continuous attention.

Now You See It...

This topic is crucial for seniors. As we age, we become more and more vulnerable to something called motion-induced blindness. It's a condition where objects can literally disappear from our field of vision.

As Dr. Comunale described, even the normal aging process causes the memory to decline, particularly short-term memory. The phenomenon can appear in remarkably subtle ways and motion-induced blindness is one of them.

In road conditions, such as while you're waiting to pull out onto a street or roadway and are scanning for approaching traffic, motion-induced blindness could cause you to miss something. The older you get the greater the chance it will happen.

I know this all sounds elementary, but as you age you've got to become increasingly aware of what's happening to you. I've been experiencing more and more instances where I thought the street or road was empty but suddenly, and alarmingly, it wasn't.

This is particularly true when I'm trying to pull out across a road and am turning left – which requires keeping track of traffic approaching from both directions. Several times vehicles have seemed to emerge out of nowhere, scaring the daylights out of me. So I've tried to compensate by looking continually to the right and left until I've completed the turn. As I prepare to pull out I act as though I'm watching a tennis match at Forest Hills or Wimbledon. Back and forth, back and forth -- for as long as it takes to get into the lane safely.

Research bears out this approach. Statistically, drivers age 55-60 have fewer left-turn crashes than any other group. But then the rate rebounds, hitting an alarming level by age 80. [59]

Mirrors, Mirrors?

If you're going to focus ahead while merging you still need to see what's coming up behind you. That can be increasingly complicated – lots of vehicles moving mean lots to keep track of.

How to simplify?

Compartmentalize your attention. First, look ahead until you're sure the ramp and the merge area are clear.

Next, scan the expressway out your side window to see what's beside you.

Last, as you approach the merge point, use your side and rearview mirrors to keep tabs on what's behind you.

Useful tip:
Think of merging this way:
    First, look ahead.
    Second, look to the side.
    Third, look behind you.

Your greatest hazard in a merge is rear-ending someone. The next, most dangerous hazard is sideswiping someone. Traffic approaching from behind is the least hazardous because those drivers can see you moving on the ramp. That doesn't mean you should ignore them; rather focus first on the vehicles you might hit – then on ones that might hit you.

Ahead, side, rear.

Don't rely exclusively on those mirrors – look!

The same goes for changing lanes. Clear the way ahead, then clear the way to the side, and then make sure the traffic behind you isn't bearing down.

Swimming with Traffic

The practice of repeatedly looking back and forth while making turns is particularly important when you're pulling out onto a multi-lane roadway. These days traffic flows just like a river, always seeking the path of least resistance. Right lane, center lane, left lane – even the shoulder – anytime there's an empty space someone is bound to slip or jump into it.

What you've got to do, essentially, is swim with traffic. How? By not assuming an open lane will stay open.

If you're trying to turn into the right lane, keep making sure somebody hasn't slipped into it from your left. I'm telling you this because I've experienced it many times. Traffic tends to fill any empty spaces that appear. Therefore you've got to check and recheck until you're sure it's safe to move.

The rule applies even in parking lots and garages. Whether you're pulling or backing out of a parking space you've got to keep looking constantly for vehicles cutting across your path. Otherwise … well, you know.

> **Useful tip:**
> When entering a crowded parking lot or garage look for a space that's empty at both ends – like the letter "H" – actually two spaces where two vehicles would be parked head to head. Pull through it and park facing the far lane. That way, when you're ready to leave, you can drive forward instead of backing out.
>   Failing that, consider backing into the space.

Beware the 'Canyon'

Looking where you're going also includes staying safe until you can look. Here's what I mean:

Say you're stopped at an intersection beside a larger vehicle, such as a delivery van or tractor trailer. As long as that vehicle blocks your view you can't know what's happening on the other side. If you dart ahead before looking you could be in for an unpleasant surprise, such as a red-light runner dashing across the intersection to broadside you.

A similar risk exists if you're moving through an intersection past a larger vehicle that is waiting to turn left. That vehicle could be hiding an unseen, oncoming driver trying to turn across your lane. Or, the intersection might be clear. The point is that you can't tell. If someone did suddenly cross in front of you, there's no way you could react in time. You'd broadside him or her at full speed.

So, if a bigger vehicle is stopped beside you at an intersection – making you feel as though you're trapped in a canyon – don't jump ahead when you both start moving again. Stay beside it until you've cleared the intersection. Let the other driver be your eyes temporarily and run interference for you.

Also, if a stopped, left-turning vehicle blocks your view, slow down as you pass it.

Never assume the way is clear.

The canyon effect can happen frequently in parking lots as well, when you're caught between two larger vehicles. Suddenly you can't see what might be rolling down the lane just as you try to pull out. What to do?

Useful tip:
If you can't see down the lane, inch your way out. Forward or backward, ease your vehicle out of the space very slowly. That way anyone, on wheels or on foot, approaching you will see you moving and be able to slip out of your way, stop to let you out, or honk to let you know he or she is coming.

Keep Looking Sharp

"Okay," you might say. "You're right. I need to look where I'm going. I need to be careful of my blind spots, and I need to watch for lane or merge jumpers. I should keep watching for oncoming traffic when I pull out of places and be careful when my view is blocked by trucks and other larger vehicles.

But those are specific situations. What do I do when I'm just driving along the road?

After a while, it becomes hard trying to keep track of everything. How do I stay sharp?"

Of course your top priority should be to keep your vision as healthy as possible.

You should become familiar with all of the vision problems related to aging and you should have your vision checked regularly. That said, no matter what your age, the best way is to use your vision naturally to alert you of hazards.

Here, my advice differs from that of some safety organizations. I've heard it recommended that while driving you should continuously keep your eyes searching out possible hazards. It's a bit like being a pilot, who has to sweep the instrument panel constantly to keep track of altitude, heading, rate of climb or descent, and so forth.

Driving isn't like flying, however, and employing an "active visual search," as the process is called, has a big problem. In my opinion it's way too much work. It will tire you out relatively quickly. Besides, no one naturally uses his or her vision that way.

Instead, use a built-in tool that will serve you well, again and again, for long periods behind the wheel: your peripheral vision. Consider it your automatic pilot. Just as in many other animals, particularly predators, we Homo sapiens have a strong ability to recognize quickly any inconsistencies in our environment.

Consciously or not, inconsistencies always attract our attention.

Inconsistencies?

Yes, things that stand out from their surroundings:

Things that contrast, either lighter or darker;

Things that are more reflective and, especially,

Things that move.

Useful tip:
In Safe Young Drivers, my book for teens and parents, I suggest the term "Ice Cream" to help them remember about inconsistencies.

> **Inconsistencies = Contrast, Reflection, Movement**
> **I = CRM. Ice Cream.**

Anything that fits into one of these categories could be trouble for you. As you drive, whether alone on the road or in traffic, the surrounding environment takes on a consistent and predictable pattern. The pavement, other vehicles, the landscape all pass by in predictable ways.

As long as these conditions prevail you can relax. Sure, check your rearview mirrors regularly and keep an occasional eye on your instrument panel, but don't expend a lot of energy actively examining every single thing that comes your way.

Let your peripheral system do it. It will automatically detect inconsistencies, which will require you to snap to a higher level of attention.

If something moves into your field of vision that doesn't quite match its surroundings, you need to focus on it quickly. Like when someone veers from the traffic flow and begins to change lanes in front of you, or when a driver signals to turn, applies the brakes, or pulls out of a driveway or parking lot. Or when a pedestrian crosses the street ahead of you. Or when a fallen limb lies on the road or broken glass litters the pavement.

There are hundreds more examples. You don't need to react to all of them. You merely need to notice them so you can determine if further action is necessary.

If you're constantly and actively searching the roadway for such hazards it becomes a case of diminishing returns. The harder you look the more quickly you become fatigued, lapsing into a lower state of attention that requires you to work even harder – which tires you out even more.

Here's an example.

If you've ever driven through conditions of limited visibility, such as fog, heavy rain or snow, particularly at night, you know how fast you can tire. In the severest case it can seem as though you must search every foot of the road ahead. This represents one of the most stressful driving situations. The stress emerges not only from the uncertainty involved – limited visibility means a hazard could appear suddenly at any moment – but also from the constant act of searching.

Though such conditions are much more severe than in ordinary driving – and they do require stricter attention – they also illustrate how exhausting an active visual search can be.

So, don't do this. Instead, achieve the same results by using your central, high-focus vision more selectively. Here's how:

First, when you start out, turn or change lanes, always look where you're going; never move your vehicle – forward or backward – into a place you haven't cleared by looking at it.

Don't move ahead without looking.

Don't back up without looking.

If your muscle tone and flexibility permit it, turn your head around and look out your back window. Rely on your mirrors only if you must.

When you're turning off a roadway, look out your side window as well as the windshield.

Don't change lanes without looking to see if someone is sitting in your blind spot.

Most important, never take your eyes off the road if there's any chance the way won't be clear. If you must look away make sure it's only for the briefest moment.

For your own sake, and the sake of everyone you care about, never forget any of this.

Second, as you're moving along always try to look well ahead, toward the horizon. Try not to stay focused on what's right in front of you – not the vehicle directly in front of you and definitely not the pavement. Its constant display of movement can create a hypnotic effect, making you drowsy or even dizzy, and possibly bringing on motion-induced blindness.

Instead maintain a relaxed, wide gaze. Don't stare. Just keep the road and the landscape ahead in your view – all of it – across your field of vision. Then, a few times each minute, glance at your mirrors to track what's behind you, and once in a while check your instrument panel to see what's happening there.

This might seem like a lot of territory to survey, but if your vision is normal you should be able to handle it. If you have vision problems watch as large an area as you can but always adjust your speed to match. Remember it's what you don't see in time that's dangerous.

Third, use your peripheral vision to pick up those inconsistencies.

If any vehicle changes its motion relative to yours, or to the other vehicles around it, whether in speed or direction, you'll notice.

If something is lying on the pavement or shoulder ahead, you'll notice.

If pedestrians, cyclists, or animals appear near the roadway ... you get the idea. Any of these things should snap you immediately to a higher level of attention.

I am convinced these tactics constitute the best and safest way to use your vision as you drive, regardless of your age. Employ them consistently and you can stay relaxed while mentally clearing the way ahead, keeping track of what's behind and monitoring what's going on with your vehicle.

Useful tip:
Be particularly aware of inconsistencies as evening approaches because they will give you the earliest possible warning of potential hazards. Something dark by the side of the road could be a large drop-off. Anything that reflects your headlights could be trouble – an animal's eyes, safety strips on bike wheels or jogging shoes, or reflectors warning of abutments or ditches. Of course, anything that moves at night should grab your attention immediately.

Useful tip:
If you're going around a curve look toward the inside of the curve – as if you were trying to look around it. You'll pick up hazards more quickly that way. Likewise, if you're approaching the crest of a hill look low over the top. And when you're in heavy traffic, try to look beyond the vehicle in front of you. That way, if something happens, say, two or three vehicles ahead, you'll be able to react to it sooner.

Useful tip:

Whenever you approach a driver waiting to pull out into your lane, watch that driver's face. If he or she isn't looking at you don't assume you've been seen. If you can't see the driver's face at all – either directly or in that person's rear view mirrors – he or she may not have seen you. You may be in a blind spot.

This is true most often with truckers, who have a lot of rig to keep track of. If you can't see them in their mirrors don't assume they know you're there. Of course, even if they have seen you, they still might pull out or change lanes into you. Keep watching until they're out of your way.

Useful tip:

The best way to tell, instantly and for certain, where another vehicle is headed is to watch its front wheels. For example, if you're moving in the right lane and a vehicle turns onto the highway from the left, you can tell whether it's going to stay in the left lane or sweep into your lane by where its front wheels are headed. Watch them; they don't lie.

Useful tip:

If you have a frequent problem with distraction, try to keep both hands on the wheel at all times. What's it got to do with looking where you're going? Two things: First, your attention tends to follow your hands. It's tough to direct your visual focus elsewhere while you're holding onto the steering wheel. Second, with your hands fully occupied you'll be less likely to handle other things such as a cell phone.

Useful tip:

If you get caught in a driving rainstorm, and you've got a pair of polarized sunglasses in the vehicle, put them on. They will help you see better through the raindrops. But do not – I repeat do not – put on sunglasses if they aren't polarized. That will just make things harder to see.

There are no great secrets here. All of these points are basic and obvious, but that doesn't make them unimportant. The proof is in how many unfortunate souls have wound up in crashes because they didn't follow the basics and forgot the obvious.

Now, as you age, they're more critical than ever.

10. Those Three Little Words
by Phil Berardelli

f you follow the two rules I've just discussed – slow down and look where you're going – you can maintain a level of safety on the road for many years. To up your safety level even more try practicing three little words – no, not "I love you," but three techniques that can likewise protect you if you practice them consistently.

React

If you look where you're going as a constant habit you'll be much less likely to run into something. There's another way collisions can happen, however: You see a hazard coming but fail to react in time. That's terrible because, as Dr. Comunale has reminded us, for seniors the consequences of a collision can be much more physically severe.

Just seeing something ahead of you – and even recognizing it as a hazard – isn't enough. You also have to take action as quickly as possible, not at the last moment but at the first moment.
`In most cases the best first action to take is a close relative of my all-purpose advice to slow down:

Get off the gas.

Anytime you spot something ahead that might require you to slow down, stop or take evasive action you should immediately remove your foot from the accelerator. Stop adding power to the engine. Whether you're moving slowly along a city street or at a good clip on the highway get your foot off the gas completely.

You won't affect your speed very much and you won't disrupt traffic behind you, but you will improve your ability to take further action safely. Almost every good driving maneuver begins with this action.

Why? Three reasons:

1. It's much easier to bring a vehicle to a stop if you're coasting instead of applying power.

2. When you're in traffic it's the least disruptive way of putting yourself in a position to stop or steer.

3. On slippery pavement it's the quickest way of regaining control if you begin to skid because you've stopped applying power to the wheels.

You must make this subtle reduction in the momentum of your vehicle in order to improve your next options. Get off the gas and you're ready for your next move, plus you've quietly communicated the need for action to the traffic behind you.

Whatever happens next – even if you simply resume your speed – will take place in a slightly calmer environment.

I can't overemphasize the importance of this approach. The longer you delay your reaction, the less safe your situation will become and the more abrupt – and possibly dangerous – the necessary maneuvers will be. So get off the gas at the first sign of any potential hazards such as the following:

1. You see traffic collecting at an exit ramp and backing up onto the highway. If you see the congestion but keep up speed anyway you'll quickly run out of room. Then you'll have to stop hard to avoid colliding with crawling or sitting vehicles. If lots of drivers around you have to do the same thing a pile-up could result.

2. As you approach a highway entrance you fail to move over or reduce speed for a merging vehicle. Or, if you're the one merging, you fail to adjust your speed to fit into traffic flow. The result: swerves and skids, rude gestures and harsh words.

3. On the open road, traffic becomes so heavy that clogs develop. Vehicles slow to a crawl even though there's no merge area or other obstruction ahead. You may see what's happening or be warned by automated traffic signs but you keep up your speed, anyway. The longer you wait to react the more severe your braking is going to have to be.

4. Road signs warn of a construction zone ahead. Instead of

slowing down and using caution you continue to push toward – or through – the zone, even if the lanes are temporarily skewed or narrowed by barriers.

5. At night on a crowded highway a cluster of brake lights is forming in traffic ahead. Obviously something is going on, yet you keep pushing, waiting until the last possible moment to slow down and consequently increasing the danger of hitting someone in front of you.

Such examples, and many more like them, are commonplace. Next time you're on a heavily traveled expressway just look at the skid marks on the pavement and the scars on guardrails and abutments. Each one is evidence of somebody who may or may not have seen a hazard ahead but definitely didn't react to it properly. That's why highways that are intermittently congested are so dangerous – because most drivers keep trying to push ahead instead of taking the most basic precautions when conditions change.

What's the difference between getting off the gas and adjusting your speed to conditions?

You adjust your speed to conditions as they are.

You get off the gas because of the possibility that conditions will change.

Is someone ahead waiting to pull out? React. Get off the gas.

Are children playing near the road? React. Get off the gas.

Is a progression of brake lights backing up toward you? React. Get off the gas.

If you can get to the point where you react this way quickly and consistently you'll find that the rest of the process comes more naturally.

What do I mean by "rest of the process?" When you get off the gas it's only a precaution, a precursor. The next step, if needed, is probably braking.

Braking in traffic is something most drivers don't do well because they tend to wait until it must be done harshly. That's what inevitably happens if you fail to react early by getting off the gas. Often it becomes too late for calm action. Instead of light braking, suddenly you're in a hard-braking, possibly emergency-steering mode. Your survival instincts must kick in. In the next few instants you must do whatever is necessary to protect yourself, even if it severely disrupts traffic flow or jeopardizes someone else's safety.

That's why it's critical to react long before the situation deteriorates. The reaction rule that applies to getting off the gas also applies to braking:

Do it at the first moment, not the last.

Anytime you see something ahead that may require you to slow down or stop – react. Do it as soon as possible.

First, get off the gas.

Then, ease on the brake.

That's the best way to deal with traffic behind you. If you react quickly and brake sooner, then your braking can be gentle. That gives the drivers behind you more time to react. It's a calming influence on traffic. It's also much, much safer.

Restrain

– yourself, that is. Get into the habit of hanging back from problems in traffic.

Restrain? Yes, keep yourself well behind the trouble. That's the best strategy for dealing with crowded conditions on the road and it's by far the best strategy for seniors to avoid collisions and pile-ups.

In today's heavy traffic you're almost always better off behind than in front.

It never ceases to amaze me when I'm on a busy highway, with all lanes occupied as far ahead as I can see, there still are drivers who insist on pushing ahead – aggressively so. They're also the ones who keep jumping lanes when traffic stalls, trying to snake their way into the clear, only to come to a stop like everyone else when they run out of room.

It's a no-win situation. The more you try to push your way through traffic the more other drivers will react to prevent you from doing so. Or, you'll provoke more drivers to push, just like you.

Either way you won't be able to stay ahead.

I recommend something closely related to reacting: Whenever you see dense traffic ahead, restrain yourself. Keep back from trouble. Maintain some distance. Allow your more competitive neighbors to battle it out for little patches of pavement. You can watch from behind and stay safe.

Examples:

1. A motorist attempts to pass a semi-trailer on an interstate but only by going a couple of miles an hour faster. The maneuver creates a moving clog, with other vehicles bunching up behind. There might be a couple dozen vehicles waiting to pass the semi as soon as the lead vehicle pulls over. If you're in this pack you're surrounded by drivers whose frustration levels are rising by the minute. Chances are everyone is packed a little too tightly together for comfort. Even if bad weather or darkness isn't involved one small mistake can cause disaster.

2. Traffic is heavy but moving. In your rearview mirror you see a vehicle snaking among the lanes toward you. Based on the way your neighboring vehicles are configured you know the lane snake is going to try to cut in front of you as well. Your instinct may be to accelerate and block the path.

3. The situation is the same, only there are two or three aggressive drivers approaching you from behind in a mini-pack.

4. You want to pass another vehicle but as soon as you begin signaling to change lanes someone in that lane accelerates to try to cut you off. You still have room to change lanes but doing so means you'll be blocking the passing vehicle, which is moving faster than you are.

In such situations restrain yourself. Don't participate. Don't provoke.

To repeat, the safest place to be is behind the trouble.

Stay out of trouble by staying behind it.

Consider the situation. Anytime you encounter a driver whose behavior is obnoxious, isn't it better to let him or her pass you by?

Then that driver is up ahead where you can watch his or her every move in safety and react accordingly. But try to move ahead and you'll have someone on your tail that could do you harm – either directly or by forcing you to make a foolish move.

An errant driver poses much less of a threat when you're behind.

The same applies to what I call pack conditions. When vehicles bunch up at high speeds pack members tend to become impatient and more aggressive. Competition begins for space and the lead.

If you want to be safe don't play that game. The best place to be is behind. Avoid getting caught up in one of those senseless, juvenile competitions that occur so often on crowded highways. Resist that temptation. Stay back. Restrain yourself.

This goes especially for you elderly curmudgeons – myself included – who can become angry at the foolishness of other drivers.

Stay back, away from them.

One other occasion is which restraining yourself is a good idea: Anytime you're sitting at the head of the line at an intersection, remember to wait a moment before starting out on the green light.

As you might know, red-light running is on the rise. Many drivers think nothing of roaring through intersections well after the light has changed. Traffic cameras have helped to curb this tendency – though they've created a new hazard from drivers who slam into the tails of others who have stopped suddenly to avoid getting tickets. But that's another story.

Don't tempt fate by moving instantly on green. Wait a beat or two; then go – after you're sure the way is clear.

Signal

Yet another basic component of safe driving – and a common courtesy – signaling seems to have been forgotten by so many drivers these days. I see it all the time.

People shift lanes or make turns without signaling.

Or, they turn their signals on during their maneuver; the vehicle essentially begins to change lanes without warning.

Or, they turn their signals on, but half-heartedly – for one or two blinks – during a maneuver.

I've even seen people turn their signals on after they're done turning or changing lanes.

All these instances are examples of FTUTC (failure to understand the concept).

Use your turn signals to alert other drivers to what you're about to do. It's an act of safety because it allows others time to react. It's also an act of courtesy because, in a sense, it's a way of saying "Excuse me but I'd like to move this way."

I've heard a lot of people say they've given up the practice of signaling because they're tired of other drivers speeding up to cut them off as soon as they begin.

Well, it's old but true: Two wrongs don't make a right. If many drivers behave rudely, plenty of others still respond courteously if you signal. Besides, it's required behavior. Sooner or later forgetting to signal will earn you a traffic ticket.

Just remember: Signal your intentions before you act.

Useful tip:
Flash your signals at least three times before you pass or change lanes, and at least five times before you merge, exit, or turn.

Remember, too, that your signals aren't some magic force field. They don't automatically keep everyone out of your way just because they're flashing. Your safety is still your own responsibility. By all means signal but never forget to look where you're going before you make your move.

11. And a Bunch More to Live By

by Phil Berardelli

My troubles are focus and reflexes. I'm too interested in too damn many things and my mind does wander. My reflexes aren't as good as those of my wife, who is seven years younger. Her reaction time is shorter. I still have one strength left, however. I make better decisions about risk, timely lane selection and the like. But I am undeniably 85. If you don't believe me, check the rate of my insurance, despite the fact I haven't made a claim in the 30 years I have been with the company.

– Gene K., 85

Those three little words (react, restrain, and signal) along with the two big rules (slow down and look where you're going) constitute the basis of a mature driving strategy. If you can adopt them as habits – even if you've never followed them before – you'll remain safer on the road.

You can do even better by fine-tuning your driving techniques. Adding to the three words, here's a baker's dozen more – plus an extra essential tip – to help keep you safe as you age behind the wheel:

Share

Author Robert Fulghum, in his best-seller All I Really Need To Know I learned in Kindergarten, talks about sharing as a basic civilized behavior everyone should learn at a young age. The idea also has importance for driving – particularly as we grow older. Our roads and highways are public places, not private domains. They serve us all best when everyone using them is considerate of everyone else – when everyone shares the road.

For seniors the concept carries special significance. As our driving maneuvers gradually slow down it becomes particularly important to radiate courtesy to the motorists around us. Good manners are catchy. If we demonstrate them at all times our fellow drivers become more likely to show patience toward us when we need it.

How to share the road? Easy. Just follow these two rules:

If someone is..., let 'em.

If someone wants to..., let 'em.

Examples:

If someone is in front of you let 'em have the right of way.

If someone is already in a lane let 'em have the lane.

If someone wants to change lanes let 'em change lanes.

If someone is turning in front of you let 'em have the time and space to turn.

If someone wants to pull out let 'em pull out.

If someone wants to pass let 'em pass.

If someone wants to cross the street let 'em cross.

If someone is riding a bicycle along the road let 'em have the space to ride.

If someone is walking along the road let 'em have the space to walk.

These are all variations on the phrase "finders, keepers." It's also a way to insert humanity into a faceless vehicle – to place yourself in the mind of the other person you encounter.

Whoever occupies a lane holds the right of way.

If you want to enter another lane either hold back and wait your turn or ask permission to change lanes – signal your intentions. If there's any doubt yield to the other person. Don't try to force your way in.

The wonderful thing about sharing is that the more you do it the more you'll want to continue because most of the time it also makes you feel better.

It's that simple: Share the road anytime you have the opportunity.

Try to act behind the wheel the way you do when you're on foot.

Wait your turn.

Allow others to go ahead of you.

Try not to step on anyone else's toes.

In other words show basic manners. Be polite – including thanking others when they're courteous to you. A simple wave or smile can do wonders to create goodwill on the road. Even if someone seems to think he or she is doing you a favor when you legally have the right of way, show your thanks anyway.

Useful tip:
When you arrive at a four-way stop sign, if there's a vehicle stopped on your right, defer to it. This is a simple courtesy that could eliminate much of the confusion at these intersections. Everybody moves one at a time, clockwise.

Useful tip:
Anytime a semi-trailer passes you, as soon as there's enough room for it to move back into your lane, flash your high beams briefly. This is a universal "all clear" signal among truckers. If it's daytime wait until you can see the driver's face in the truck's rearview mirror so you can be sure the driver sees your gesture.

Whenever I do this, many truckers flash their running lights back at me to say "thanks." That's a welcome return, a trucker sending a friendly greeting your way. It means, for the time you and that truck will be traveling in proximity, the driver will become your ally. On today's roads you need all the allies you can get.

Steer
Sometimes your two hands can be more effective than your right foot because some dangerous situations can appear too quickly for you to stop:

You're rounding a blind curve when you encounter a speeding oncoming vehicle that has crossed over the center line.

You're heading along a straight stretch of two-lane highway

when someone in the oncoming lane drifts into your lane.

You're moving next to a semi-trailer that begins to change lanes into you.

You're driving along a city street when someone pulls out of a side street directly in front of you.

You're driving on a street alongside a row of parked vehicles when a child darts out between two of them or someone in a parked vehicle suddenly opens a door.

In such examples, and many more, what you do in the next few seconds will determine whether you end up with only a case of jangled nerves or a dented vehicle and injuries.

For many drivers their first instinct would be to hit the brake pedal. In many cases, however, that instinct would be wrong. Why? Because braking takes time, and hard braking can cause loss of control.

A better bet is to steer your way out of trouble.

Steer? Yes. Get off the gas, of course, but at the same time instantly and reflexively change the direction of your vehicle. Head it away from the trouble.

Useful tip:
Steer to daylight. It's a variation on the way football players learn to run with the ball: toward the nearest opening on the field. That is, don't focus your attention on the object you're trying to avoid. If you do, as counterintuitive as it sounds, you'll tend to move toward it. Instead, ignite your peripheral vision. Look for the biggest, emptiest space in front of you and steer toward it. Then keep steering until you're out of trouble.

Ease

As I keep repeating, the older we get the more time we need to maneuver our vehicle safely. I'm not talking minutes, of course, but even an extra second or two can make a big difference when reaction times are involved. So, whenever you're in traffic, the more gradual you make your maneuvers the better. That goes for lane changing, passing, merging, and turning.

Here's what I mean:

When you're changing lanes make the maneuver a smooth and steady transition, not an abrupt one.

When you're merging ease into the traffic flow, moving approximately the same speed as traffic. Don't force yourself onto the highway. Don't lag, either, something that requires other drivers to swerve around you or slow way down.

When you're exiting, signal first, and well before the off-ramp. Ease onto the deceleration lane and then slow down.

When the traffic light turns green, gently press the gas pedal to bring your vehicle back up to speed gradually. Except for the idiots – excuse me, I meant maniacs – among us, as long as you continue to accelerate, even moderately, the drivers behind you will be fine with what you're doing.

As mentioned, when slowing down first get off the gas and let the vehicle coast then apply the brake gently. If you stay on the gas longer and brake more severely you'll still end up at the same spot, but it's less safe and harder on your vehicle.

Maintain

I'm not talking about changing your oil. Yes, maintenance is important, but my point here is about speed and position. Wherever you go, maintain a steady speed and stay in your lane as much as possible.

Watching traffic these days makes you wonder if most drivers think lane-changing is some kind of sport. Then there are the drivers who can't seem to hold a steady line. Even when they're not changing lanes they're weaving back and forth within a lane.

This kind of behavior contributes heavily to the chaotic nature of our highways. It's dangerous because it's unpredictable – and it's particularly dangerous to seniors because lots of background activity can become confusing. When bunches of vehicles continually change their relative positions, no one can be sure what anyone else is going to do at any given moment.

There may not be much you can do about the behavior of drivers around you, but at least you can boost your own safety by becoming steadier.

Try also to maintain a steady and smooth line within your lane. Follow the course of the road. If you have trouble doing this it may be because you aren't looking far enough ahead or, possibly, you're not holding the steering wheel properly.

There's an emergency situation that requires you to maintain your speed and lane, at least temporarily: a tire blow-out. This can be a frightening experience because it almost always happens suddenly and unexpectedly. When it does the usual tendency is to brake hard and try to steer off the road immediately.

That's the worst thing you can do. Such an action could throw your vehicle dangerously out of control. If you're driving a van or SUV – something with a higher center of gravity – you could even roll it over.

If you have a blowout, and feel your steering wheel being tugged to one side or the other, the first and most important thing to do is get off the gas. Stop adding power to the wheels. Then steer a straight heading within the lane until your speed drops to the point where you feel you can pull off the road safely.

By the way, anytime you have to pull off the road remember this:

Always pull off as far as you can safely. In today's environment the farther away from other moving vehicles the better.

You might ask, "If you want me to stay in my lane, which lane is best?"

In general – and no surprise – the right lane is the best lane for anyone driving at or under the speed limit. Just about everyone is willing to give other drivers the right lane. Also, staying to the right prevents most speedsters from passing you on the right.

There's a complication with the right lane, however. It has to do with merges, which have become among the most dangerous spots on the highway. If you stay in the right lane it will sometimes place you in the center of the most chaotic traffic. I suggest a compromise: Stay in the right lane, but if you approach a merge area that's congested move over one lane until you've passed it.

Think

Good driving is mostly sensing and reacting but thinking is essential, too, especially thinking ahead. It means, for example, determining well beforehand what lane you need to be in so you can exit, merge, or make a turn, thereby avoiding doing anything at the last moment.

"Rats! There's my exit! I've got to swing across now!"

It's just common sense. If you know an exit or turnoff is coming up on the right, and you're in the left lane, don't wait. Move into the right lane as soon as possible.

Then, making the turn will be simple and safe, instead of frantic and dangerous.

THE MOST DANGEROUS

Let me digress just a bit. I regard one driving situation as the most consistently dangerous we face: passing on two-lane roads and highways – particularly those with speed limits of 55.

The statistics support my opinion. Mile for mile, two-lane roads produce the largest number of fatalities and serious injuries. It's easy to understand why. They present a constant danger of head-on collisions, as vehicles traveling in opposite directions pass within a few feet of one another and, during passing maneuvers, oncoming vehicles actually share the same lane.

Two vehicles traveling toward each other at 55 miles an hour are moving together at a combined speed of 160 feet per second. That's a football field in less than two seconds and a mile every 33 seconds!

Therefore, passing another vehicle on a two-lane highway requires very clear thinking and judgment – and lots of visibility.

If you can't see at least a half-mile down the road, don't try it.

If you can't judge how far a half-mile is, don't try it.

If the vehicle in front of you is moving at or near the speed limit, don't try it.

If you must pass, however, and the above caveats don't apply, then do so with extreme caution, making sure your headlights are on – which should be the case anytime you're traveling on two-lane roads whether or not you need to pass other vehicles.

What about when someone begins to pass you on a two-lane road? Extend that driver the courtesy of slowing down so he or she can move back in front of you more quickly, and flash your lights as soon as the vehicle is clear to move over in front of you.

Suspect

Safe driving relies on a quality that has been taught for many years: defensiveness. It's something that's been expressed in a slogan used frequently in highway-safety advertising:

Watch out for the other guy.

The concept is similar to one used by bicyclists to promote safe riding. It's called being an "invisible rider." That is, always suspect that a driver can't see you or isn't looking and then base your actions accordingly. The same applies to driving. Protect yourself by not trusting others on the road. In other words:

Suspect the other guy (or gal).

It isn't rudeness; it's self-defense. It's an attitude that doesn't require you to take any action against another driver. You only have to make certain you can proceed safely no matter what that driver is doing:

If you're waiting to pull out and a vehicle is approaching with its turn signal on, suspect that the signal has been left on inadvertently. Don't move until the driver slows down and actually begins making the turn.

If you're approaching a vehicle waiting to pull out, and if the other driver isn't looking at you, suspect that he or she hasn't seen you and therefore may pull into your path. Even if the driver is looking at you, suspect that he or she will still pull out suddenly.

If you're merging onto a highway, suspect that traffic behind you won't move over or slow down to let you in. Give yourself plenty of time and room.

If you're following another vehicle, suspect that the driver isn't fully alert. Keep back a safe distance in case he or she makes a mistake or has to stop suddenly.

The full list is lengthy. Anytime there's a situation in which another person can act unsafely and put you in jeopardy, suspect that's what he or she will do. Take precautions so if the worst does happen you won't be caught unaware.

Bottom line: Don't trust anyone else on the road. At least don't presume any action by anyone else. Treat other drivers as guilty until proven innocent. Suspect they won't behave properly until they demonstrate otherwise.

This is a subtle but critical point. Defensive driving becomes increasingly critical as we age. Suspecting other drivers is simply a way of keeping your guard up – of being totally responsible for your own safety.

Observe

Another way of keeping yourself safe from other drivers is to observe the way they behave. You can tell a lot about the skills and attitudes of others very quickly if you pay attention.

I'm not suggesting that you observe every other driver. It's too much work, it will bore you, and it will tire you out quickly. Instead employ your peripheral vision, concentrating on the drivers who attract your attention. Usually they will fall into one of the five categories I call the "Imps" of the highways:

Impatient. Probably the easiest to spot, this driver is always pushing to get ahead, tailgating, snaking in and out, trying to gain advantage and jumping ahead at merges. This person is also the most likely candidate to be what I call a slicer. That is, someone who will close fast on you from behind in the left lane, pass you, and then cut across your path right at an exit. So ease up a little and let the impatient so-and-so by.

Remember, you're always better off behind a bad driver than in front of one.

Impervious. This is someone who isn't paying enough attention to the road or traffic conditions. The vehicle isn't holding steady in the lane. Maybe it even drifts into another lane. The driver runs stop signs and red lights or sits for a long time after lights turn green. It could be a case of temporary distraction because somebody is switching radio stations, talking on a cell phone, chatting with a passenger or texting. The driver also could be oblivious to anything but the immediate road ahead. Maybe the driver is simply so timid that he or she can't handle more than basic moves. Whatever the cause this behavior is disruptive. You would do well to steer clear.

Impulsive. This driver will tend to pull out in front of you suddenly or will change lanes without warning or seemingly without reason. This is a difficult character to spot because the behavior is so unpredictable. It could appear at any time. Once you see someone act impulsively, though, assume he or she is likely to do it again.

Impudent. Here's someone whose behavior is similar to the impatient driver's, but with attitude. This person actively wants to take advantage of others. He or she communicates a "stay away from me" attitude and tolerates nothing that seems to be a challenge from anyone else. My advice? Let the angry souls have their space.

Incidentally there's a peculiar characteristic among impudent male drivers I've observed for many years: They tend to lean to the right while driving. They steer with their left hand, rest their right hand on the gearshift knob or center console, drop their right shoulder, and keep their head upright. I call this posture "the Lean."

Next time someone passes you in a way that suggests arrogant or angry behavior, check his posture. Chances are the guy is doing the Lean.

Impaired. This driver needs no introduction. It's someone who's responsible for a huge toll in life, limb, and heartbreak. In this day and age, after so many years of public service campaigns warning about the dangers of mixing driving with alcohol or drugs, some people still get behind the wheel while impaired.

The sad thing is that many impaired drivers are difficult to spot until it's too late. If you see anyone acting under the influence, report it to the police.

All five types of drivers, in their own ways, are menaces to everyone else on the road. Given enough time and bad luck they risk ending up being "imps" in five other ways: impacted, impaled, impoverished, impounded, or imprisoned.

Watch out for all of them. Their danger is contagious and we can't afford to catch it.

Read
You might often feel alone out there on the roads, but highway safety engineers are doing their best to accompany you. You can see their signs everywhere – literally, displayed in bright colors with large type and a few simple words. They've been placed for a reason: to give you information you need to keep safer.

So, read the signs, obey the ones that display traffic laws and pay special heed to those that give warnings, such as at railroad crossings.

Hundreds of people, drivers and passengers alike, die needlessly every year because their vehicles are hit by trains at crossings. Fully loaded trains have stopping distances measured in quarter-miles, not feet. Anyone unfortunate enough to be caught at a crossing in front of a moving train has very little hope of surviving.

So, do your utmost to avoid such a horrible prospect:

Never try to cross a railroad track unless you can see that the track is clear in both directions.

Never try to squeeze under a crossing gate when it's closing or opening.

Never try to cross a railroad track unless the road on the other side is clear.

At ungated crossings with no warning signals, after the train has passed, wait until you can see far down the tracks in both directions before attempting to cross. Another train might be approaching on a different track, which you couldn't see or hear because of the first train.

Something else you should read: the label on any medication you're taking.

Alcohol and illegal drugs aren't the only substances that can impair your driving. Prescription drugs can have the same effect. Many medications carry warnings not to drive or operate machinery whenever you take them. These include some of the most popular products to treat colds, the flu or allergies.

If you're taking any medication make sure it doesn't carry a warning not to drive.

Wait

Many tragic situations could have been avoided by waiting even an extra second or two. Crashes at intersections, for example, though declining in recent years, remain a significant hazard. [60]

At other venues, hasty moves into traffic disrupt the normal flow and often force other drivers to brake hard or even swerve to avoid collisions. Jumping ahead at merges and exits has helped make those sites highly chaotic.

Chaos causes crashes.

Don't pull out into traffic if doing so will disrupt the flow. Wait a little longer. There's always a better break in traffic just a few more seconds away.

Wait your turn when entering or exiting. Give the driver in front of you time and space to merge safely. After a merge, if you want to pass, wait until you're in the traffic lane and have a clear passing lane.

Once again, when the light turns green, wait a moment before starting out. Make sure crossing traffic has stopped. You don't want to cross paths with a red-light runner.

Also as mentioned, left turns become more challenging as we age. So when you're trying to turn left in front of oncoming traffic make sure there's plenty of time to complete the turn and get out of the way. How can you tell? Check your rearview mirror after you've cleared the turn. If three seconds pass before you see traffic cross in your mirror you've made the turn safely.

It's even more critical to wait anytime you want to turn left in front of an oncoming motorcyclist. Many people have trouble judging the speed of motorcycles. Their smaller size and narrow profile make it difficult to tell how fast they're approaching. Too often, people will turn or cut across a cycle's path, believing they had plenty of time, only to be shocked by a near miss – or a collision.

Be just as careful about bicycles. They don't travel nearly as fast as motorcycles but their riders can suffer serious injuries if they tangle with vehicles. Wait. Give bicycles plenty of time and plenty of room.

Illuminate

Announcing your presence on the highway is important for safety. Other drivers need to know you're there. They need to see you easily. The best way to be sure about this is to illuminate your vehicle. Drive with your headlights on.

Many of us might remember the days when it was actually against the law in some jurisdictions to drive with headlights on during the day. Fortunately most jurisdictions have become more enlightened – excuse the pun – allowing lights on at any time. Also, many newer vehicle models are equipped with daytime running lights.

What most new vehicles do have – which has become an inadvertent problem – are daylight sensors that turn the vehicle's lights on automatically. Many of these sensors aren't sensitive enough. They don't activate the lights until the skies grow quite dark.

I began to notice this a while back. As evening skies approached, I saw a sizeable percentage of vehicles still without their headlights on – between 10 percent and 20 percent by my rough calculation.

If you've become a senior driver, or are nearly there, you can remember when you used to have to turn your car's lights on manually. Nowadays, because of lingering imperfections in the system, you need to keep turning them on:

Turn them on when skies darken and it begins to rain or snow. Some states now require you to turn your lights on anytime you have to use your windshield wipers. Law or not it's a good idea.

Turn them on anytime you notice most of the approaching vehicles have their lights on. Chances are they're moving out of bad weather and you're moving into it.

Turn them on as soon as the sun sets. No, you won't be able to see the road any better, but other drivers will be able to see you much better.

Turn them on anytime you're driving on a two-lane highway with a speed limit above 35. Oncoming drivers can see your headlights much sooner than they can see your vehicle.

Turn them on anytime you're approaching or driving through a construction zone. Highway workers need to see you quickly, too.

The critical thing to remember about lights is it's just as important for you to be seen as for you to see. Remember to illuminate yourself anytime your visibility diminishes or you need to make your vehicle more conspicuous.

Useful tip:
Worried about leaving your lights on and running down your battery? First of all, I don't know of a single vehicle model these days that doesn't come equipped with an audible headlight reminder, which activates if you open your door with the engine off and the lights on.

But if the alarm is missing, or if you can't hear the reminder, no problem. Get in the habit of looking back at your vehicle after taking a few steps away from it. You'll notice whether your lights are on and can turn them off long before your battery loses its charge.

Listen

Use your ears as well as your eyes to gather a lot of important information about your safety on the road:

Sirens on fire engines, ambulances and police cars;

The sound of an approaching train at a crossing;

The warning blast of another vehicle's horn, and

Possible trouble with your tires or other parts of your vehicle.

The quicker you become aware of these things the quicker you can react to them. That means keeping the ambient noise down inside the vehicle. Don't crank your radio volume so loud you can't hear what's going on outside and don't allow conversations to distract you.

Most important: Have your hearing tested periodically, so that if you're beginning to suffer hearing loss, you can take steps – yes, such as wearing hearing aids – to compensate for it.

Ungrip

Remember I started this section talking about reassessing your driving habits?

Here's one: Where do you hold your hands on the steering wheel? If it's on top you've got some unlearning to do.

Gripping the top of the steering wheel means one of two things:

Your arms are extended too far and too high from your body, or

You're sitting too close to the wheel.

Extending your arms accelerates fatigue, because holding them that high for long periods is tiring. Sitting too close to the wheel restricts your arms from moving quickly in an emergency. Both positions encourage tension, because people who keep their hands on top tend to grip the wheel too tightly.

Both also risk breaking your hands, arms or face if you're involved in a crash and your airbag deploys.

One hand at the top is even worse. It has all the previous disadvantages plus it provides less control in an emergency.

If your habit is to drive one of these ways make no mistake; you are jeopardizing your safety and the safety of your passengers. You need to retrain yourself.

Where should you keep your hands? I recommend the "No Lunch/No Dinner" rule: Keep your hands away from the zone that's equivalent to 11 to 1 o'clock (lunchtime hours) if the wheel were a clock face. The same goes for the bottom of the wheel. Stay away from 5 to 7 o'clock (dinnertime).

Instead, keep your left hand somewhere between 8 and 10, and your right hand between 2 and 4. In both cases, choose whatever is comfortable and easiest, depending on how the outer wheel is attached to the center post. Chances are you'll readjust your seat to a better distance away from the wheel as well.

Unsteer

Here's a minor item. Do you steer improperly when you park? I'm not even talking about not placing your vehicle in the center of parking spaces. I'm talking steering when your vehicle isn't moving.

When you're parallel parking, do you back into a space until you're up against the vehicle behind you, turning your wheels while sitting still? Then do you move forward, stop, turn the wheels again, move backwards, stop, turn the wheels, and so on?

When backing out of a parking space, do you move into the clear by only a few feet, stop, and then tug on the steering wheel until you're headed in the right direction?

When trying to turn around in tight quarters, do you repeatedly work the steering wheel while stopped?

If that's your problem, Bunky, as I said it's a minor item. Nevertheless, turning the wheel while the vehicle is stopped rubs flat spots into tires and wears out steering components. When you're stopped, don't steer – hence, "unsteer." It takes just a little concentration and practice to do things properly:

Whenever you're in a tight spot you can move into the clear more easily and quickly if you remember the "extra turn" maneuver. Whether you're moving forward or backward, before you stop, always turn your wheel in the next direction you want to go.

If you practice this consistently you'll always be in a better position to make your next move. You'll soon be in the clear without subjecting your vehicle to unnecessary wear and you'll keep other drivers waiting less – always a good move.

> **Useful tip:**
> When you back out of a parking space, keep backing out until you're well clear of the space – as far back as you can practically go. Then you'll be ready to pull away more quickly and easily.

That Essential Extra Tip

I assert this as someone who has changed a flat tire by the roadside probably a dozen times over my driving lifetime: If it isn't an emergency, or unless there is absolutely no alternative, don't do it anymore. Call your emergency roadside assistance provider and have them summon a properly equipped and trained professional. Or, if you don't currently subscribe to one, through the AAA, your vehicle's warranty package or your auto insurance company, do so.

Changing tires has always been a risky proposition, but these days it's become downright dangerous.

For one thing, you stand better than a remote chance of being hit by a passing vehicle propelled by a distracted driver.

For another, carmakers have taken to storing spare tires in increasingly inaccessible places – for example, on my Chrysler Town & Country minivan it's suspended under the floor panel beneath the front seats. To get at it means crawling under the vehicle.

One more: It takes a lot of strength to loosen lug nuts that have been fastened with air wrenches.

Perhaps most important, with our aging bodies become more vulnerable to injury by the year, it isn't worth exposing ourselves to danger when safer alternatives are readily available.

Maybe leave this task to the pros.

12. Stay Cool, Be Happy

by Phil Berardelli

I retain some sense of humor about senior drivers, but not much. They aren't that funny. Obviously I am exposed to the risk of encountering drivers like myself. On a recent trip to Florida I was newly amused by a bumper sticker I had seen before: "When I get old I'm going to move up north and drive slow."

— Gene K., 85

My colleagues and I have written this book to help you be safer on the road. This chapter maybe will help you enjoy the process a little more – even if you've been at it, like me, for half a century or more.

The harsh reality of today's American highways is that every time you drive you're likely to encounter many situations that can raise your frustration and rub your nerves raw. Part of it emerges from the sheer barrage of noise and commotion you have to contend with. Very quickly on the road your senses can become overwhelmed. Fatigue is also rampant among drivers.

Part of it also is caused by the foolish and rude behaviors that have become so prevalent to the point of being unavoidable. You can't escape them and you only have two choices when you encounter them:

Give in to your own negative emotions.

Find ways to stay calm and detached.

Obeying raw emotions behind the wheel endangers you and everyone around you, making you part of the problem. Diffusing them makes you and everyone else safer, making you part of the solution.

Stop Hurrying, Stop Worrying

Back in the late 1950s, sociologist C. Northcote Parkinson invented a concept of behavior he called Parkinson's Law:

Work expands so as to fill the time available for its completion.

In simpler terms, if you have two days to finish a job you'll take more time to do it than if you only have a few hours. There's a variation on Parkinson's Law that works for driving:

The more you hurry the longer the trip will seem.

The corollary is: The less you hurry the shorter the trip will seem.

I don't remember exactly when I discovered this but it works. I used to hate sitting at stoplights, as most of us do. Then one day I was on my way to conduct an interview in the city and I needed to brush up on some background material about my subject. Every time I reached a stoplight I'd pick up the material and scan through it as quickly as possible, thinking I could put the wasted time to good use.

A funny thing happened, though. Suddenly it seemed as though the lights were changing back to green in just a few seconds. No sooner would I start reading than the light would switch again. I actually became frustrated because the red lights weren't lasting long enough!

I've tried the same strategy several times since, with the same result: Red lights seem much quicker if you distract yourself from them.

Please don't misunderstand: In no way am I advocating that you carry reading material for the times you're stopped. For one thing it's not exactly a pleasant experience. Instead of being frustrated because you're not moving you become frustrated because you can't finish a paragraph before you have to move. For another, if you forget about the light, and it changes, suddenly you're blocking traffic. As we know well, there's no worse crime on the highways than blocking someone else's path.

My point is that much of the tension and frustration we experience on the road is caused by our effort to hurry. By the same token these feelings can be reduced or eliminated if we simply stop trying to hurry.

What else can you do to make the driving experience as pleasant as possible? Continuing the keyword approach I used in the previous two chapters, here are my suggestions:

Apologize

This may be the most important thing you can do whenever you tangle with another driver over something that is your fault. An immediate, clear gesture of apology from you to someone who believes you did wrong can stop plenty of problems before they start. People may remain angry for a while, but if you simply admit fault nearly everyone eventually will calm down and release their ill feelings about you.

> **Useful tip:**
> What kind of gesture can communicate apology clearly? If you're moving the best one I can think of is to hold up one hand, wave and nod your head a few times. If you're stopped, hold up both hands. You might even want to mouth "Sor-ry," in two big syllables as well. It's non-threatening, accepting and good manners. It works all the time for me. In a couple of cases people were downright surprised to see somebody admitting a mistake. They actually smiled.

Forgive

Giving forgiveness when someone else is at fault is just as important as seeking it. Most behavior on the road is inadvertent. Even if someone else is rude, let it pass. Mistakes happen. You make them, and so does everyone else. Be generous with your forgiveness. Remember the Golden Rule. It's an oldie but goodie.

Connect

Sometimes a little bit of human interaction can diffuse a potentially tense situation or simply make another driver feel more comfortable. Much of the selfishness and hostility on the roads can be traced to drivers who forget that other drivers are ordinary human beings just like they are. People tend to respond well to friendliness and not well to rudeness.

Whenever you can, make positive connections with other drivers. Smile, wave, nod or even shrug, depending on the circumstances, something that suggests you acknowledge them as people, and respect their presence on the road.

Break through the impersonal nature of the highways and force some realization that a human being inhabits your vehicle.

Enjoy

We've all been driving for so many years that it's common to forget about the experience of driving itself. We tend to become preoccupied with reaching our destinations. So maybe it's time to return to the pleasures we enjoyed during our first few years behind the wheel.

Jessie Thorpe will explore this aspect memorably in the book's last chapter.

By all means always watch the road. But also pay some attention to the scenery. If you look where you're going properly, you can still notice the houses, buildings and landscape that go by. You can also amuse yourself by observing other motorists.

The point is to allow yourself to be more open to the sights and sounds of your journey – within the process of keeping your eyes on the road ahead and on the traffic around you. The two activities aren't mutually exclusive. You can find pleasurable things to notice on trips you make frequently – even every day.

I've discovered over the years that no matter how many times I travel the same route, if I stay aware of the landscape, I always detect something new. I'll see a pretty home for the first time, or a garden or a tree. Whenever I do I take delight in the new sight. Just the other day, I saw a lovely home in my own neighborhood, something I had never noticed before. I smiled at the realization.

Something else can be true, too: You can enjoy re-encountering familiar things.

There's a house along the Pennsylvania Turnpike that never ceases to amaze me. It's situated near the banks of the Juniata River, just east of the Midway rest stop, between the Bedford and Breezewood exits. It's a modest, completely ordinary house, drab even – except for one thing: It sits at the base of a wooded, steep mountain slope stacked with hundreds of boulders.

Every time I pass that house I marvel at its precariousness. If the three most important words in real estate are "location, location, location," the builders of this place either weren't listening or decided to defy conventional wisdom.

It isn't a new house; it has occupied that site for many years. Yet it seems so vulnerable. If one of those boulders ever started rolling down the slope behind it there would be nothing left of the place except splinters. Each time I catch a glimpse of it I smile and wish its occupants well for their courage and maybe foolhardiness.

That's how enjoyable driving can be if you let go of your fixation on your destination. Don't discount the experience itself.

The experience inside your vehicle can be pleasant, too. If you're traveling with someone, have a conversation. Nothing makes the miles go by more quickly. The process of dialogue won't distract you – if you follow one simple rule: Keep your hands on the wheel. Don't begin gesturing while you're talking. That's what leads to distraction.

Keeping your hands properly on the wheel will prevent you from diverting too much attention to the conversation. You'll enjoy the best of both worlds: staying safely alert and using the verbal interaction to melt away the miles.

Useful tip:
If you're alone, particularly at night when you can't see the scenery, the next best thing to a conversation is listening to talk

radio. The back and forth of voices will not only draw your attention away from the monotony of the road, but it also will stimulate your alertness. Music has the opposite effect – even loud, harsh music. Avoid it when driving at night. Choose human voices to keep you company.

Rest

Sometimes, drowsiness appears no matter how much you try to distract yourself. That's why, as we age, it's critically important to confine our driving to manageable stretches.

A good rule is to break for 5 or 10 minutes every two hours, then half an hour or so every four hours. Stop, get out of the vehicle, stretch your legs, walk around, use the restroom, buy a snack, whatever. It's important to boost your circulation and clear your mind of the inputs and stresses of driving.

If you become really tired stop driving altogether. Get off the road. Find a motel and get a good night's rest.

Useful tip:
Can't find a motel or absolutely need to keep going? Pull into a rest stop or designated roadside area for a while. For your safety find a place that's well-lit and busy (when you're exhausted from driving the light and noise won't matter). Turn off the engine and shut your eyes. Even a 10-minute or 15-minute catnap will help. If the drowsiness returns repeat the process at the next available stop.

Don't deny your body the rest it craves because the longer you fight drowsiness the more severe it will become. A drowsy driver is just as dangerous as a drunk driver.

Repeat: A drowsy driver is just as dangerous as a drunk driver.

By the way, there's another reason why it's important to stop and stretch your legs periodically: It can help your circulation, something that becomes essential as you grow older.

Immobility is the enemy of circulation and in some cases it can aid the formation of a deep vein thrombosis, also known as a DVT – a blood clot in the lower leg. I know about this condition because I've suffered through it twice. Take my word for it; you don't want one. It's difficult to overcome and if you don't notice that it has developed – the most obvious symptom is swelling in your calf – it can kill you.

Snack

One sure way to bring on drowsiness is to eat a big meal before driving or eat a big meal during a long trip. Doing so forces your body to work hard to digest the food and that restricts flow of blood to your brain. That's why you always feel sleepy after you've had a big lunch or dinner.

You need to pace yourself during your drive. Have smaller and more frequent meals. If you don't want to spend the time or money eating at restaurants carry some food with you. The point is to wait until your journey is over before eating a full meal.

Drink

Or, more properly, hydrate. How you drink is just as important as how you eat. Sitting in a vehicle – particularly during sunny days – can bring on dehydration, which hastens fatigue. You can counter this by keeping a bottle of water with you and drinking regularly. You don't have to keep buying new ones. Give the landfills a break and reuse the car-sized container. Keep refilling it from a larger jug or your tap. The main thing is to get into the habit of maintaining a food-fluid intake while you're driving.

Yes, drinking more water will require you to make more rest stops, but as I said, that isn't a negative factor. Getting out of the vehicle every couple of hours and stretching your legs helps fight fatigue. For the diet-conscious, taking in water tends to make you less hungry, which means you'll be less likely to be tempted by fast food establishments along the roadside.

One obvious caution: Don't sip water while you're moving

unless the way ahead is clear, the road is straight and there's nobody else around you.

Exercise

Until engineers invent a vehicle that can drive itself – and, yes, I know Google is already using one for its Google Earth street maps – we'll need as much physical skill as possible behind the wheel. Driving requires the near-constant use of our hands, arms and feet, and it demands the ability to turn our heads to the right and left. So, as long as we drive, we need stamina and flexibility.

That, in turn, means keeping ourselves as fit as possible. In fact, the Mayo Clinic, in its 7 tips for older drivers, tops the list with a recommendation that seniors stay as physically active as possible, particularly by performing strength-building and flexibility routines.

In an earlier chapter Lidia Wasowicz Pringle cited a study touting the benefits of walking around a track for 40 minutes a day, three times a week, for keeping your brain – and hence your driving consciousness – healthy. [61]

Driving is not, and never has been, for couch potatoes.

Appreciate

Once in a while, as you're traveling our nation's highways and byways, your local streets and roads, and even lanes and alleys, think about all the planning and hard work it took to build and maintain them and all the people who do that work.

Appreciate the fact that for most of our long lives it has been possible to go from any place in America to just about any other place simply by getting in ours vehicle and driving there. Even the most remote regions are accessible to some extent by road.

Although we all complain about the time we spend in our vehicles on our highways, we couldn't maintain our lifestyle without them. They are the arteries that carry not only us but also the lifeblood of our society: our food, clothing, furniture, consumer electronics, mail, household supplies – a cornucopian bounty.

Modern life would be nearly impossible without our network of streets, roads and highways, and the bridges and tunnels that allow them to run continuously across mountains, valleys, rivers and other bodies of water. How much more complicated our journeys would have been without that paving of America, the fruits of the labors of thousands upon thousands of our countrymen.

How blessed we have been.

13. Meanwhile, Technology Is Riding to the Rescue

by John Matras

Nick the barber is intrigued by the rearview camera in the minivan parked outside his shop. "I'm not very tall to begin with," he says, "and I'm not able turn my head and look over my shoulder like I used to. So yeah, that would be a good idea."

Nick's complaint is a common one. Dr. Comunale has detailed how, as we get older, we don't bend like we once could. And it isn't the only thing. Comedian Jeff Foxworthy calls it "ustacould." Our eyes aren't as sharp, our night vision isn't what it was, and our ability to change focus from near to far goes away – hence the dreaded bifocals. We're not as spry (the very word makes one shudder), and our reaction times have slowed down, too.

The good news is that new technologies are helping to counter our declining faculties to some extent, via certain features increasingly available on new cars. The rear-view camera is just one, though it isn't expressly designed for senior drivers.

Everyone can benefit from the camera, which gives a view of areas otherwise blocked by the vehicle itself, particularly in a minivan, SUV or pickup truck.

Extra Eyes and Ears

In the case of the rearview camera, the device is usually housed in the bezel around the rear license plate. It displays an image either on the dashboard screen used for the navigation system and other functions or, in vehicles without those screens, on a smaller display on one side of the inside rearview mirror.

Some of the newest vehicles offer enhanced rearview cameras, adding superimposed lines on the viewing screen to help the driver gauge distances. In some cases the lines bend with the turning of the steering wheel, showing the path of the car if the wheel continues to be held at that angle.

Other new and available technology and features can make life behind the wheel easier for the no-longer-quite-so-young crowd. More extensive systems add multiple cameras, including minicams under the side mirrors. They can spot what would otherwise be out of sight, such as a small child or other short object. Some vehicles feature a camera that adds a panoramic front view, making it easier to stick the nose of the vehicle out of enclosed spaces, such as urban parking garages, where pedestrians and traffic may be out of sight for the driver.

Senior status notwithstanding, backing out of mall parking spaces can be daunting, particularly when you're positioned between two minivans or an SUV and a pickup truck. Side-looking sonar – which uses sound echoes, similar to the pinging used to detect submarines, though inaudible to the human ear – can detect oncoming vehicles and warn the driver.

Even basic sonar devices, which have been around for a decade, can warn of an obstacle lurking behind the vehicle, their audible beeps increasing in frequency as the car moves nearer to it, and augmented by a series of lights above the inside rear window or even projections onto the navigation screen. The devices also can detect how close objects are to the front or rear corners of the vehicle.

Once I was driving down a progressively narrowing "old city" street when the beepers for both front fenders started going off. Fortunately, the car had a back-up camera, so I could edge my way back out.

Speaking of corners, technology can help you see around them, so to speak, penetrating the vehicle's blind spots. Often these can be relatively large zones, and inevitably another driver will find one of them to be a perfect camping area, doing everything but pitching a tent. A new device called a blind spot monitor – though typically each manufacturer has given it a name of its own

– can detect a car, truck or motorcycle positioned where you can't see it. The system warns you with a visual alert, typically a light on the A-pillar, on the base of the outside rearview mirror, or on the face of the mirror itself. Some systems add an audible warning, or a brighter flashing light, if you signal for a lane change.

Keeping Your Distance

New models are using radar for "intelligent cruise control." It improves on regular cruise control by keeping your car at a constant speed but slowing to maintain a minimum distance from a vehicle you're approaching from behind. The intelligence quotient is useful, but it also can be annoying for a driver who's perfectly aware of his or her surroundings.

Intelligent technology now extends to braking, in the form of systems that will take over if a vehicle's sensors and onboard computer calculate that a collision is imminent. As with cruise control, there are drawbacks. Intelligent braking must distinguish between objects in the vehicle's path, moving or not, whether the closing speed presents a danger, and whether the object is close to the vehicle's apparent path.

Volvo has developed an advanced system that uses cameras to detect human forms and apply braking automatically to eliminate or mitigate hitting an errant pedestrian if the driver isn't paying attention. The system bows out if the driver brakes or takes evasive action.

Wandering drivers also can be aided by sophisticated camera-based systems, detecting whether you're drifting over a lane marker or paint stripe along the side of the road. When the image seen by the camera doesn't match what its programming says it should see, the steering wheel vibrates. Infiniti offers a system that will even tug the steering wheel to nudge your car back in line. (Using the turn signal automatically deactivates the system. Or, it can be turned off at the driver's discretion. But then why have the system and not use it?)

Some of the higher-end models now offer night-vision systems, which use infrared or light-enhancing technology – though low "take rates" have discontinued their availability in Cadillac, for example. One problem: The systems typically display images on the vehicle's instrument panel, requiring the driver to split attention between the screen's depiction of the road and the actual roadway ahead.

It's all too tempting to drive by the infrared image alone, but there's a lot more going on than what you can see on a flat, white-on-black screen.

Automotive 'Granny Glasses'
It had to happen. Carmakers, aware of the increasing number of senior drivers, have begun using larger fonts for instrument panels, so now car shoppers can judge the ease of reading not only the lettering on the gauges but also the controls, various knobs and buttons, and even touch screens. Be sure to try them not just in the daytime but also at night.

That's just the start in what's likely to become a wave of features and accessories for the senior-driving set. For those experiencing difficulty shifting their gaze between the road and the instrument panel, manufacturers are offering "heads up" displays, or HUDs, which project primary information onto the windshield and require a less-frequent change in focal length. The information includes speed, turn-signal indicators, navigation-system instructions and more.

Super Peepers
It might seem obvious, but for night driving the quality of headlights becomes more important for seniors. The more the road looks like it does in daylight, the less night driving seems like night driving. Fortunately, a new generation of headlights is making that quality easier to achieve.

A general rule is that halogen is good, projector beam is better, Xenon better still and Bi-Xenon best of all. Xenon projects a bright light with a midday color spectrum (and a sharper beam cutoff so it doesn't blind oncoming drivers).

Another new development: LED headlights. LEDs, or light-emitting diodes, not only are bright but also emit a spectrum of light that is very close to daylight – which our eyes have evolved to see – making it easier to travel at night.

Incidentally, whenever you see the phrase "Xenon headlights," it generally means low-beams only; high beams are usually some version of halogen, and they show how bright and white the Xenon lamps are in comparison. The term "Bi-Xenon" means the vehicle uses Xenon for both low and high beams.

Also new: active headlights. Based on a concept developed nearly 65 years ago by Preston Tucker for his automobile of the same name, active headlights perform like blind-spot monitors. Going by different names from different manufacturers, the lights pivot in the direction the vehicle is turning. How much and how quickly the lights move may vary by manufacturer and model, and typically by how fast the vehicle is going and how much the steering wheel is turned.

I've tried them and they're addictive. Going back to standard headlights makes you feel like every corner is an adventure into a black hole.

None of this is cheap, however. Xenon headlights, for example, can add a thousand dollars to a car's sticker price; active headlights even more. But don't test-drive these features if you don't want to buy them because trying them will convince you otherwise.

Assuming the Position

Another factor that determines how well you can see the road ahead is the height of the driver's seat. Simply put, sitting higher means you can see farther and around and over traffic, possibly giving you a critical edge in reaction time.

Your seat position is part of your car's ergonomics, the measure of how much work it takes to accomplish a task – something particularly important for seniors.

Improved ergonomics means the car can adapt more to the reduced mobility of older bodies. One well-established way has been to provide a multi-adjustable seat, which features not only a seat bottom that can be elevated and moved fore and aft over a wide range, but also a backrest that can be set at many different angles and an adjustable lumbar support to improve comfort during longer drives.

Something that's been around for a while but remains important for seniors: power-adjustable pedals, which can also help tailor a car to a particular driver.

Massaging seats, by the way, are almost sinfully delicious to one's derriere. If comfort promotes safety, why yes, massaging seats can be considered safety devices – and as good an excuse for having them as any.

Against the Grain

One modern trend in automotive design has been working against our aging bodies. It's the practice of making new models more and more aerodynamic to reduce wind resistance and improve fuel efficiency. All well and good, but sleek and low-slung new models are making it more difficult for the less limber of limb, and it's not simply a matter of being able to sit down and stand up from a seat of a given height.

Many new models feature more steeply raked windshields that can make front-seat entry and exit more difficult not only for a driver but also for passengers.

Alas, the car industry is showing no signs of reversing this trend, so it's important when choosing a new vehicle to test its ease of access – in both the front and rear seats. It's also a recommended practice not only for senior drivers but also those who transport elderly passengers.

Stopping Short – of Crashing

Automakers have come a long way with braking systems as well. More powerful brakes can significantly shorten stopping distances and mean the difference between a scare and a collision. In addition, an antilock braking system, or ABS, can shorten stopping distances in low-traction conditions by preventing skidding.

It might seem counterintuitive, but locked-up wheels and sliding tires won't stop a car as quickly as rolling tires that still have traction.

ABS is now standard on more cars than not and should be considered a must for drivers of all ages – even more so for seniors. ABS will not overcome the laws of physics, of course, and low-traction surfaces will always create longer stopping distances, antilock brakes or not.

Stability control takes ABS a step farther. By selectively applying brakes individually, stability control – which goes under different names by different manufacturers – helps a car resist plowing off the road or spinning. It's no cure-all but it's a help for all drivers, particularly those whose reaction time isn't as sharp as it once was.

A new feature rapidly becoming standard is called brake assist. Again, different carmakers use different names for it, but the concept is the same. A sensor monitors how quickly a driver takes his foot off the gas pedal and applies the brake, and then determines whether a driver is in a panic-braking situation.

Studies have shown that, contrary to what might be expected, drivers of all ages often don't use full braking even during emergencies. But brake assist applies the brakes fully when it detects a panic situation, thereby reducing stopping distance and the likelihood of a collision.

All you need to do is hope the vehicle behind you has brake assist as well. As a safety feature, brake assist disengages as soon as the driver releases the brake pedal completely.

Many of the features and systems available on the newest vehicles are making driving easier for younger drivers as well as seniors. But those improvements become especially useful for drivers as their abilities begin to decline.

Nick the barber's next car may well indeed sport a rearview camera. And even more.

14. A Farewell to Driving

by Lidia Wasowicz Pringle

I have good eyes, good health and a good driving record, and I drive a good car, the Prius V, but I do occasionally think about when I will no longer be able to drive, which I hope is not too soon. I am more cautious, careful, slow and aware than when I was young, and I'm always non-drinking when I drive. I'm a safer driver than I was when I was young, driving a sports car and in love with speed. There's no question of doing that now!

– Willi B., 81

On a sunny afternoon in 2010, as her car chugged up the steep sliver of a street snaking its way to her house on Belvedere Island, 88-year-old Judy Wallerstein expertly maneuvered a hairpin turn – and came hood-to-hood with a cement mixer.

There was little to do but back down to a short stretch of road wide enough to let the colossal truck pass without slipping into a ravine.

"These roads were built for horses and carriages, not for cement mixers," notes Wallerstein, who in her younger days thought nothing of driving 70 miles to have her hair done. "After I had trouble backing up because I couldn't turn my head enough, I decided I didn't want this nightmare."

Although she has perfect vision without glasses, a valid license and a pristine record of no moving violations in the past 60-plus years, Wallerstein now leaves all of the driving to her husband, who just turned 90 and, accident-free, had his license renewed for another four-year term without having to take a road test.

"My children didn't tell me a thing," Wallerstein declares.

"I gave up driving on my own."

It was a deliberate but not premeditated decision.

"I don't think people think ahead about giving up driving," she says. "It was a goddamn nuisance, but did it break my heart? No."

Mary Rogers, 94, who as a bride put some serious miles on the odometer chasing her Navy husband across the country, is equally sanguine about her retirement from driving six years ago. Neither a collision nor near-miss nor anything out of the ordinary drove her to it. Rather, as she was heading home along the aptly named Paradise Drive one uneventful morning, a thought suddenly darted in front of her.

"I was driving and I said to myself, 'If nothing strange happens, I'm okay. But if something comes along out of the ordinary, I don't think I can manage it,'" she recalls. "And I said, 'That's it.' So, I made the decision myself."

A natural-born financial whiz with a head full of common sense, Rogers had prepared for this day her entire working life. And it paid off. By the time she was ready to hang up her car keys, her savings and investments – compounded over the many decades she had spent in the workforce – sufficed for her newfound needs.

"I went to the fellow that runs the gym (where she works out), and I told him that I [needed] help getting there, and just then a lady came in looking for employment as a caregiver," relates Rogers, a self-made success story that started when she had to fend for herself at age eight. "We got in touch, and she was hired the next day, and from that time on, I had drivers."

The former broker acknowledges it took a full tank of fiscal responsibility and forethought to fuel the change in course that kept her independent life from sputtering to a stop.

"My passion is managing money so I have financial resources. I can hire the best of caregivers, which I have, so that one lady does a lot of driving for me, taking me back and forth to exercise class, and the other lady comes in three times a week three hours a day, and she bathes me and cooks and cleans and keeps me up to date," divulges Rogers, who has weathered a series of financial storms since starting to squirrel away a portion of her pay in the 1950s. "So that's how I handle the senior driving."

Too many may handle it by overextending their road life, she charges.

"Yesterday I am down in the parking lot of Kaiser (Permanente Medical Center), waiting to get a prescription I needed, and I see a car drive in with a handicap placard, and a lady gets out needing some help, which I understand, and the driver gets out – an ancient, feeble man, and he's the driver!" she exclaims. "I thought, 'Oh my God! He's going to go out on the road again! Aye yai yai!' Also, twice a week, I go down with [a friend] and we exercise, and I see the people coming in there, and some of these drivers scare me to death."

Rogers thinks such drivers are not realistic about their ability to navigate the roadways safely, but she also understands that not everyone has her resources or resolve.

"I've still got it up here," asserts the retired financial planner, tapping her forehead with long, slender fingers. "And … because I've saved and saved and saved and invested wisely, I have enough money that I can hire help."

She tries to assist friends whose driving days are numbered, though not all pay heed to her advice. One pal in particular dreaded reaching the end of the road.

"That was a big deal for her, and she was in panic mode," Rogers remembers. "I said, 'All right, you tell me exactly how much it costs you to operate your car for a year, and I want you to put that in $20 bills and stack them up. Now, every time you need a ride, call a taxi, and there's your money. Easy. Physically, you can see it.' But she didn't. The number-one problem was she didn't know how much it cost her because she didn't keep records … Her daughters finally took the car away."

To avoid such a fate, it pays to recognize the warning signs and know when to exit voluntarily, as Rogers and Wallerstein did.

"If you worry about your driving safety or if a family member or doctor suggests you stop driving, it probably is time to give up the keys," advises Virginia G. Wadley, the clinical psychologist

I mentioned earlier who is also a professor, program director and specialist in gerontology, geriatrics, dementia and aging and mobility at the University of Alabama at Birmingham. The National Institute on Aging sees red if you answer "Yes" to any of the following questions:

Do other drivers often honk at me?

Have I had some accidents, even if they are only "fender benders?"

Do I get lost, even on roads I know?

Do cars or people walking seem to appear out of nowhere?

Have family, friends or my doctor said they are worried about my driving?

Am I driving less these days because I am not as sure about my driving as I used to be?

Do I have trouble staying in my lane?

Do I have trouble moving my foot between the gas and the brake pedals, or do I confuse the two? [62]

John D. Locher, the senior-driver advocate with the California DMV, adds the following signs that your time in the driver's seat might be expiring:

Feeling uncomfortable, nervous or fearful while driving;

Finding dents and scrapes on the car, fence, mailbox, garage walls;

Ignoring traffic signals;

Speeding or driving too slowly;

Braking late;

Having difficulty judging gaps in traffic, concentrating at the wheel or turning your head around to look over your shoulder, and

Suffering physical or psychological conditions that could make driving hazardous.

Waning memory ranks high among those, says Matt Gurwell, the retired Ohio State Highway Patrol trooper who founded a national organization, wrote a workbook and developed programs aimed at helping older drivers stay safely on the road and, when the time comes, transition to life after driving.

He cites the tragic story of an elderly Pennsylvania couple freezing to death because they forgot their way home from their daughter's house and wound up stuck in a farm field 60 miles from their intended 40-minute route. [63]

"There is also the problem of drivers with memory lapses providing an excellent target for someone up to no good," he warns from experience. "The criminal sees the perfect target in a confused older lady who pulls into a gas station to ask for directions because she's lost. Memory is an extremely important element of safe driving."

Although forgetfulness and certain other impairments typically tie into age, skill alone should determine whether a driver has reached the end of the road, Gurwell emphasizes. He describes a common telephone exchange:

Hello, I'm from Des Moines. My mom turned 80, and I don't think she should be driving.
Why not?
Well, she's 80.

"The daughter's intentions are good," Gurwell says, "but she's clueless about her mom's physical driving abilities. The thinking is: 'Someone turns 80, so that should be the last day he or she drives,' when there is no justification for this in real life."

Psychology professor Norman Abeles of Michigan State University also cautions against jumping to age-based conclusions.

"While senior drivers tend to have more fatalities when they do have accidents, by and large, they are safer than 20-to-25-year-olds," he attests. "Several years ago, we tested a driver who had the sixth worst driver's record in our state. We found no neuropsychological deficits and concluded the problem was most likely a personality disorder affecting that person's driving."

"Driving ability should be assessed for each individual and

should not be judged simply by age alone," Abeles urges. In fact, no state restricts mature drivers solely on that basis. [64] The widely ranging limitations that do apply have some critics calling for more uniformity as older drivers hit the road in record numbers and travel more miles than ever before. [65, 66]

In a survey of 2,422 men and women ages 50 and older, 85 percent of respondents who were 75 to 79 years old, 78 percent of those in the 80-to-84 age group, and 60 percent of those over 84 listed driving as their usual means of transportation. [67]

Often lumped into the "riskiest driver" category with inexperienced, testosterone-teeming teenage boys, seasoned drivers, in fact, have lower per-capita rates of police-reported crashes. [68]

On a per-mile-traveled basis, however, the percentages start accelerating at age 70 and rev up considerably after age 80, as Dr. Williams reported based on data compiled by the Insurance Institute for Highway Safety. [69]

The AMA cites motor-vehicle crashes as the leading cause of injury-related deaths among 65-to-74-year-olds and second only to falls in the 75-to-84 age group. [70]

Per mile driven, the death rate for vehicle operators older than 84 exceeds by nine times that of sturdier drivers ages 25 to 69, who are less likely to suffer from the bone-brittling effects of osteoporosis or atherosclerosis of the aorta, which can rupture when the chest smacks against an airbag or steering wheel, as Dr. Comunale described and according to the doctors' group. [71, 72]

If such considerations make you feel it's time to have the facts-of-driving-life talk with your parent, think through the psychological, physical and pragmatic ramifications before you begin, experts advise. [73]

An end to driving can trigger or worsen isolation, depression, physical decline and deterioration of qualify of life, and it can hasten entry into a nursing home and even death. [74]

Wadley sees surrendering the car keys as "tantamount to giving up the checkbook – a real blow to self-esteem and contrary to the American ideal of independence."

The blow to autonomy strikes with particular vengeance at the self-reliant warriors who beat back the Depression, the Dust Bowl, World War II and the Korean War, notes Dr. Donald J. Iverson, the Eureka, California, neurologist whose patients include retired drivers with depression.

"Don't forget these are the folks of 'The Greatest Generation,'" Locher reflects. "They saved the world in World War II, they built greatness into this country, and now they are no longer self-sufficient and not even capable of going where they want when they want! This is a huge emotional blow."

It was for Iverson's 94-year-old grandfather, who racked up millions of miles as a racer and drove to Nova Scotia on a whim at age 85 before the family confiscated his car.

"He didn't react very well to being told it was no longer safe for him to drive, but he was getting forgetful and was oblivious to speed," Iverson recalls. "We sold his car. That's how we got him to stop driving."

Getting patients with dementia to stop driving requires extra skill and sensitivity, observes the neuroscientist who wrote the guidelines for handling such cases.

"The diagnosis is the first of many blows the patient and family will have to endure," Iverson empathizes. "It brings up discussion of myriad unpleasant topics, including end-of-life care, assisted living, conservatorship, all of which need sensitive handling."

Iverson stresses that "dementia erodes the very essence of the person, his personality, autonomy, ability to socialize, and this must be considered. It's dehumanizing, an awful, relentlessly progressive and usually incurable condition."

Whatever the state of mental health, he adds, forking over the keys "is an admission of mortality; it's a huge deal."

Tackling such a tender topic may require the finesse, fortitude and fearlessness of a NASCAR driver.

"The importance of driving, especially in this culture, has many implications, including the challenges adult children face as they try to talk with parents who are in denial or are failing," says Dr. Rita Ghatak, director of Aging Adult Services and Geriatric Health at Stanford University Medical Center in California.

"There aren't too many of us around that are trying to integrate preventive measures as well as seeing patients on a daily basis," adds Ghatak, who heads several programs dealing with cognitive impairment and effective screening for the elderly. Yet these issues "are so critical."

During home visits and family meetings, she's found that "driving is a very difficult topic not only for aging adults but also for adult children coping with their parents."

Gurwell has seen the issue split families apart.

One adult daughter, one of nine siblings, became so troubled by the family feud that she was willing to forgo her inheritance to end it.

"She said, 'Dad, take me out of your will, but give up driving. You've no business driving anymore, and I'm tired of the bickering,'" Gurwell relates.

To prevent such friction, the DMV will gladly take the fall as the "bad guy," Locher says. "We're used to it, and if it serves to keep the family together, we don't mind."

Family unity, in fact, is essential for successfully negotiating a settlement with the retiring driver.

"If the adult children don't agree on how to handle the situation, or at least present a picture of uniformity during the discussions, it won't go well," Gurwell warns.

Renegades should show restraint, those experienced in the process insist.

"You don't want one person to sabotage the message by siding with the driver," Wadley points out. Nevertheless, "it is important to acknowledge to the 'retiring' driver that you recognize how difficult this decision is for him or her."

Just how difficult it is may depend on the driver's gender.

"When you have to give up driving, it's an entirely different experience for the man and the woman," maintains Wallerstein, who taught family, child and adolescent psychology for 26 years at the University of California, Berkeley.

For the typical female, driving represents her freedom; for the male, his manhood, she says.

"Giving it up is a tremendous blow psychologically for a man," Wallerstein contends. "It's a blow to a woman when she's not independent, but it doesn't have all the sexual connotations that it has for a man."

She advises against going into gender neutral when attempting to shift drivers' attitudes toward road retirement.

Women can take a direct, though kind and gentle, hint, Wallerstein says, offering, "Maybe it's time, Mom," or, "It's not a good idea, Mom," as seemly starters to the conversation.

"Independence is very important, and you hate to impose on your friends all the time, so the end of driving is very serious for women," Wallerstein states. "On the other hand, if I can't back up when I see a cement mixer, I can't, and that's the end of the discussion."

With a man, in general, the messaging needs a bit more massaging, she opines.

"You have to keep in mind the man's pride is at stake," Wallerstein says. "It's very insulting to be told, 'Daddy, you're getting old; I don't think you can drive anymore,' and it does not endear that child to the father. Is there a kind way to do it? No. Is there an unkind way? Yes."

A positive and progressive spin can blunt the inevitably heavy blow to the man's ego, she explains.

"It has to be done in terms of all the things he can do, and it has to be done in stages," Wallerstein advises. She offers some sample opening lines that can turn off or tune in the listener.

Turn-off: *Dad, the way you drive gives me the shakes. You're going to kill us all someday.*

Tune-in: *It's wonderful, Dad, that you can (insert skill one) and that you can (insert skill two), but we have been getting more and more* *concerned about some of the hazards of driving, and we'd hate to have you feel that you might be responsible in an accident.*

Turn-off (a common one): *I've watched you drive, Dad, and it is a disaster waiting to happen.* (or) *Have you seen the doctor, and what did he say?*

Tune-in: *You've been such a responsible person your whole life, Daddy. Have you thought there might be a time when you might not want to drive anymore?*

Turn-off: *My friend was driving behind you, and she said you hardly stayed in the lane!*

Tune-in: *Have any of your friends decided what to do about driving? What have they decided? Have you talked to anybody about it?*

The final note: Give him the sense that control lies in his hands, that he's in charge, by including phrases such as, "Have you thought?" and "Have you talked?" and set the speedometer on slow and steady, Wallerstein recommends.

The observations apply less to the younger generation that is just starting to hit its senior stride.

"Traditionally, females tend to accept giving up driving easier than males do because, historically, driving had been the 'man's job,'" opines the DMV's Locher.

"Of course, this has changed, and as baby boomers become the new seniors, this will not be the case."

Judy Mark, for one, has a number of friends who happily leave the chauffeuring to their wives. In part, they concede, they do so because of the women's superior skills at the wheel. They admit, however, they don't mind in the least delegating the designated-driver duties, Mark says, laughing.

A general rule of the road to retirement for drivers of both genders states a preference for an incremental shift to the passenger's seat.

"You don't do it all at once at the last minute," Wallerstein instructs.

She recommends starting out with tactful suggestions that the driver stay away from the city or keep off the roads at night or avoid the airport, then gradually extending the limits to wider areas and circumstances, as safety considerations warrant.

"The real key is not just dumping this on someone all at once," Locher agrees.

Thus, it's never too soon to start driving the point home.

Gurwell advises adult children: "No matter where your parent is right now, generate a casual conversation about driving tonight, even if saying no more than, 'Did you see how that elderly couple froze to death? Guess they got lost.' Open the door to talking about driving today."

Then proceed with care, caution and a comprehensive proposal for alternative transportation, experts suggest.

"When family members approach the senior driver, it is paramount that they already have some plan for mobility and how the senior will now get around," Locher stresses. "Having a committed mobility plan in writing with assurances that socialization, shopping, church, doctors and other outings won't end is essential."

Some alternatives to driving include:
Carpooling;
Dial-a-ride and paratransit systems provided by senior centers, hospitals, independent or assisted-living communities;
Delivery services, such as for groceries or medications;
Friends and family;
Low-speed vehicles, such as scooters or golf carts;
Non-emergency medical vehicles;
Scheduled bus and van services, whether municipal, community or organization-sponsored;
Subways, taxis and trains;
Volunteer drivers from church, community centers, schools or synagogue, and
Walking. [75]
"In the event that your patient must cease driving, the transition from driver to non-driver status will be less traumatic if he/she

has already created a transportation plan," the AMA notes. [76]

If the plan involves use of an unfamiliar mode of transport, family members might want to go along for the ride a few times to ease fears and facilitate the transition, DMV officials recommend. [77]

They should also postpone selling the vehicle, if possible, because most seniors feel more comfortable going to appointments in their own cars. [78]

Pointing out the practical gain of switching off the driving might lower the emotional toll as well.

"Detail the price of gas, insurance and vehicle maintenance for a year [to] demonstrate that ... transitioning to alternate mobility options may result in a huge financial benefit," Locher advises.

And point out that the savings can now be used for something else, says Irene Hulicka, distinguished professor at the State University of New York at Buffalo, whose expertise centers on adjusting to aging, the fears of the elderly and psychological services for seniors.

"When you approach it from the positive point of view – 'Think of the trouble you'll be spared: no more changing tires, no more changing oil, no more removing snow from the driveway' – they take it better," she promises. "You have to be sympathetic because not being able to drive anymore is a very big loss, but when you approach it from the point of view of how much money, time and trouble they'll be saving, it goes much better."

Among numerous government agencies and private enterprises putting in their tankful's worth on how to make it go much better, the National Highway Traffic Safety Administration recommends three key steps. [79]

Briefly stated, these include:

1. Collect information from personal and others' observations of the senior's driving skills made while riding in the car or following the vehicle at different times of day, in various types of traffic and under an array of road and weather conditions. Record any general risky behaviors, such as forgetfulness, disorientation,

dizziness, shortness of breath, and trouble with coordination or movement.

The file also should contain the driver's scores on self-assessment exams, such as the AARP's "Test Your Driving IQ" or the AAA Foundation for Traffic Safety's quiz. Obviously, don't delay handling anything that poses an immediate danger, such as running red lights.

2. Develop a plan of action for how the senior will get around in the post-driving days. Select a family member or friend the driver trusts to present your concerns, supported by the information you have gathered, in a sensitive, nonthreatening manner, using the first person: "I am worried," rather than "You can't drive."

3. Follow through by involving the senior at every turn and reviewing the plan of action at least twice a year to ensure it continues to serve its purpose. [80]

What works for one family, of course, may not do for another, and the plan may stall a few times before it starts purring along.

"In some cases a frank discussion with the driver will be all that is needed," Wadley observes. "In others, the family members may have to appeal to authority, enlisting the help of the physician or DMV or both. There are many cases in which individuals lack self-awareness or deny difficulties, and resistance to giving up the keys is monumental."

"When all else fails," she says, "deception or diversion can have a place in the arsenal of strategies. Many older adults have been allowed to save face through the use of creative tactics."

When stuck, turn to the DMV to tow you out, implores chief senior-driver advocate Charley Fenner, citing a case where an older man reported his own grandchildren to the authorities when they took his car to keep him safe.

"The grandparent, who really was a danger on the road, knew who did it but still called the police," Fenner says. "It does not matter that their heart was in the right place; what they did was 'grand theft auto.'"

The man's grandchildren got off with a warning after returning the vehicle, but another officer might not have been that accommodating, he cautions. The family should have contacted the DMV, which declines anonymous referrals but will keep family names confidential, Fenner states.

The previous day, he had helped out a frantic caller, concerned about his 85-year-old father's short attention span and erratic driving. First, Fenner assured him that few seniors, himself included, are entirely immune to wandering focus.

"I have to concentrate on my driving and steering, making sure I'm in the right position," Fenner, 73, admits. "I'm not able to sightsee as I used to when the whole process of driving was on semiautomatic."

An overview of the situation, however, led him to recommend a trip to the doctor's office for memory and cognitive testing and an unbiased assessment. He offered to break the news to the father, who has Alzheimer's, but the son decided to handle it himself.

California issues limited, typically one-year, licenses to patients with mild dementia but draws the line as the brain disorder progresses.

"If the doctor says it's moderate or severe, the driving days are over," Fenner explains. "Clearly, we'll see more and more of those cases as people live longer."

The next day, he received a call from a dialysis-center worker reporting three elderly patients she deemed unfit to drive. "We're careful about how we handle such information," Fenner says, noting one woman had turned in 10 of her neighbors as "dangerous drivers" because, it turned out, she wanted a better parking space.

In cases that warrant license revocation, Fenner stresses his desire to prevent harm. "At times, it's the 75-year-old, not much older than me, and sometimes the 90-year-old who's having trouble," he says. "I've had some people lose a license who were younger than me. If I need to be the bad guy and take the license away, I can do that. I take no pleasure in it, but it's part of the job."

Iverson, the neurologist, feels the same way.

Reporting drivers or recommending they get off the road "is not a responsibility that we seek out, but it is part of the commitment to the greater public good and patient health," he says. "We're not policemen, but we have a legal and moral obligation."

Research shows patients recognize and appreciate that obligation. [81]

One survey, in fact, indicated physicians hold more sway over older drivers than do their relatives. Although a family's recommendations have only "limited influence," a doctor's advice "is the most frequently cited reason that a patient stops driving," the study3authors report. [82, 83]

Yet, many primary-care physicians shudder at the thought of having such a conversation. "A lot of doctors don't want to deal with it so will refer patients to specialists like me," Iverson discloses.

The reluctance may stem from an unwillingness to deliver bad news and face the resulting resistance or resentment, fear the angry patient may switch to another doctor, or sympathy for someone about to lose driving benefits – valid concerns all, the AMA acknowledges. [84]

"In Eureka, I know the entire medical community, so I know who wants to handle the driving issue and who wants me to handle it," says Iverson, who manages such matters with extra-soft kid gloves.

"I handle it delicately because I have a tremendous respect for the people of this generation and what they've been through, what my generation hasn't had to deal with: world wars, the devastating dust storms of the 1930s, the Great Depression. I respect their self-reliance. I respect their autonomy."

As Wallerstein and Rogers demonstrate, these need not cease at the end of the road to driving. Even then, there may be light at the end of the tunnel.

15. There's Light at the End of the Tunnel
by Lidia Wasowicz Pringle

I won't give up driving until my keys are taken away! Recognizing that that may happen someday (I'm already curtailing night driving), I'm planning ahead, looking at home locations where all the necessities are within walking distance. In the meantime, I try to stay physically and mentally active to keep on driving – and to keep up with my 15-year-old granddaughter. I belong to three adult discussion groups to brainstorm about these issues. It's better to prepare than be caught unaware.

– Jim M., 79

For Judy Wallerstein, a stop to driving didn't put a dent in her American lifestyle. Since she voluntarily hung up her car keys a year ago, following that earlier-described encounter with the cement mixer, her social and socially conscious calendar has brimmed with engagements.

"I gave up driving; I didn't give up living," the 89-year-old dynamo asserts. "I do everything else. I go out. I see friends."

She also runs interference for senior causes and, most recently, worked to bring a forum on independent living to her town, which has no mass transit and a large population of residents past their 65th birthday.

Wallerstein, who leaves the driving to her husband and the shopping to hired help, recognized the need for such a gathering after doing extensive legwork with a group of friends interested in in-home services for seniors. The seminar, sponsored by a local nonprofit with a mission to help older adults live on their own, delved into how to seek, select, supervise and if necessary switch suitable caretakers.

Wallerstein correctly predicted a full house for the panel discussion, knowing her community's demographics and noting "a new movement in America for seniors to remain in their own home rather than enter a nursing facility."

The AARP made the same observation in a 2010 survey of adults 45 and older, 86 percent of whom voiced a preference for staying put as time goes by. [85]

Wallerstein relates to that majority, having given up driving rather than move to a more easily accessible address that would not require backing down a steep, skinny, squiggly roadway when a cement truck comes along.

"I decided to live in my home on Beach Road, so I have to pay the price," says Wallerstein, who wouldn't have it any other way.

Neither would Mary Rogers, who, six years into her retirement from driving, is harvesting the fruits of her lifelong labor.

"I am 94 years old," she muses, pausing to take in the scenic view of the San Francisco Bay and skyline and through the picture windows in the home she's lovingly turned into a museum of her mementoes. "It's quite remarkable, the shape I'm in, and I know it."

She eagerly anticipates the arrival of her caretaker and the start of the project they have planned for the day.

"Saturday and Sunday, we're going to can my recipe for chili sauce," Rogers enthuses. "I sit in the chair with the book in my hand, and she does all the work. She is loving it as much as I am. We can, and we cook, and we make cookies. We have a great time."

As with retirement from the workforce, the exit from driving need not lead to a deserted lot, assures Max Gurwell, author of a workbook for older drivers and their families that maps out ways to stay safe on the road and to make a smooth transition when it's time to get off.

He details the clever course a Michigan couple took to ease the husband's dreaded move to the passenger seat. They traded in their two vehicles for one to serve them both, eliminating any resentment that might ensue from the wife keeping her car but taking away his. And they purchased an automobile the husband long desired, making the transfer not just palatable but pleasurable.

"He was so happy, he bragged to everyone who would listen that he had a personal chauffeur to drive him around in the car of his dreams," Gurwell recalls. "He thought it worked out in his favor."

When the wife's turn came to turn in her keys, she couldn't turn off the tears.

"She cried and cried, saying this was the toughest thing she had to face since the passing of her husband," Gurwell relates.

Two months later she gushed with excitement.

"I'm busier now than ever since I gave up driving," she told Gurwell. "All my friends, neighbors, and my church know I no longer drive, and the phone rings all day long. I have to turn down invitations!"

A similarly pleasant surprise was in store for Rogers's friend after her daughters put an end to her driving.

"The strange part about it was that she was renting a lovely little apartment with all of her treasures around, and she had no help at all and was managing well," Rogers remarks. "She shopped and cooked, and her daughters would come in and clean up."

Until they decided it was time for mom to retire from the road and took her car, accelerating her entry into a retirement facility.

"A month later, I go over, and she says, 'Mary, I thought that I was happy in my other home, but I'm really happy now!'" Rogers laughs at the memory.

Five retired drivers, five satisfactory solutions. Is yours far behind?

Assistance may not wait at every turn, but there might be more than you expect around the bend if you take the right road, the sages surmise.

"Try not to equate driving cessation with being put out to pasture," urges Virginia G. Wadley, the expert on aging and mobility at the University of Alabama at Birmingham.

"Don't give up social activities, doctor appointments or religious services. As a non-driver, you might be able to promote the development of acceptable driving alternatives for yourself and others," she points out. "There also are many activities, services and resources available through the internet and/or home delivery. You can expand your world significantly without getting behind the wheel of a car."

Now's the time to keep busy in other venues, learn to stay independent by using alternate modes of mobility, develop a new interest or hobby or take on a cause, suggests the California DMV's senior-driver ombudsman John D. Locher.

Volunteer with an organization that provides transportation to the elderly, work with social-program advocates who call lonely shut-ins, take bus trips with senior groups, join clubs that offer frequent outings and provide rides, he advises.

"What will happen to the 85-year-old who thinks, 'If I can't drive anymore, I'm going to die,' versus one who says, 'I'm going to figure out a way to play cards with my friends on Tuesdays?'" Gurwell asks rhetorically.

Any healthy retirement plan must include ways to keep up schedules and spirits, he stipulates.

As an added bonus, studies suggest positive thinking may play a powerful part in protecting older adults from pain, stress and illness. [86]

All for an optimistic outlook, the AMA directs physicians to help patients see the pluses of abdicating the driver's seat and steer them away from discussion of such negative aspects as loss of independence or surrender of freedom. [87]

Among benefits to keep in mind, the savings on car maintenance, gas, oil, insurance, parking fees and tickets can now go toward other uses, including private or public transportation, Wadley notes.

"Giving up driving does not have to mean a loss of independence," Gurwell contends. "All it means is we have to figure out another way to get them there, even if it might be inconvenient."

During his group workshops and private sessions, he promotes creative thinking. "Ask the older driver, 'What's your goal – to have your hair done Tuesday morning or to drive to the hair appointment?'" he advises families. "'Because if it's just to have your hair done, we can solve it.'"

To fulfill the promise, the family must have the means and mindset to keep it.

"You can't just say, 'Hand over the keys,' and leave," Gurwell instructs. "There are families who handle it that way, but these are your parents, and they're owed more than that."

Families should provide the retired drivers with a written schedule of where they'll be going and who will take them, "so they can hold, see and feel something tangible that they can plan around," recommends Charley Fenner, the California DMV's senior-driver ombudsman-in-chief.

And they must bring the older relatives "into their mind frame before they cease driving so there is no 'cold turkey,'" he adds.

The AMA recommends The Hartford's "We Need to Talk" and "At the Crossroads" brochures for working out a program of outings, activities, errands and a plan to handle each trip. [88]

Families also can assist in arranging special deliveries of groceries, newspapers, medications and other needed supplies. [89]

Those who, for whatever reason, do not wish to rely on family or friends can choose to use public transit or walk, though these may not provide suitable alternatives, especially in areas of limited or non-existent availability or in circumstances that call for door-to-door service. [90]

The U.S. Department of Health and Human Services offers Eldercare Locator, either online at www.eldercare.gov, or by calling 1-800-677-1116. The service can provide contact information for the local Area Agency on Aging, Alzheimer's Association, and other organizations with comprehensive lists of senior-specific transportation resources.

Acknowledging the inadequacy of current offerings, particularly in rural areas, legislatures and non-government entities are investigating and implementing programs to help non-drivers reach their desired destinations. [91]

For example, United We Ride, a federal interagency initiative, aims to serve the transportation needs of people with disabilities, low incomes and senior status.

The safety net of support services should be cast far enough to enfold everyone willing and able to help – from family, friends, neighbors and religious groups to civic organizations, government agencies, nonprofits and private enterprise, experts advise. [92]

"There may be more ways to get around than you think," the National Institute on Aging proclaims on its Web page covering senior drivers. These include free or discounted cab or bus rides for older adults in some communities and carpools that don't require all participants to have a vehicle.

To meet the growing need for workable transportation solutions for mature adults, entrepreneurs are calling up extra reserves of American ingenuity. Among these, Monika White, of the nonprofit Wise and Healthy Aging in Santa Monica, California, responded to that 2003 tragedy in her town, in which an 86-year-old man smashed his Buick into a packed farmers' market. [93]

She collaborated with filmmakers at Wiland-Bell Productions to create a 30-minute documentary, "Getting Around – Alternatives for Seniors Who No Longer Drive," as well as a companion Web site, www.getting-around.org. A key stated aim: "Expanding everyone's travel options through improved public transportation and new models for mobility."

The Beverly Foundation of Pasadena, California, in conjunction with the AAA Foundation for Traffic Safety and several other organizations, has produced a brochure, "Supplemental Transportation Programs for Seniors." Its purpose is to survey leading local programs that help seniors transition from driving to relying on alternative transport means.

"Community planners are beginning to adapt to a future that will be dictated by the needs of aging baby boomers," Wadley observes.

Their job would be simpler if the car wasn't such a driving force in American culture.

"My friends in London have cars, but they don't drive in London," Wallerstein notes. "They take the metro, as do our friends in Paris. Weekend driving. That's what you use the car for in London and Paris, but not in America, where the whole mall development concept is predicated on cars. We Americans have one car, two cars. When our children get older, we get three cars. It's ridiculous."

Wadley agrees.

"Our society has a lot to learn from other societies in which the automobile is less central to independent living," she acknowledges. "This is a public-health issue that should be brought to the forefront of daily news and conversation. All disciplines should be involved in promoting safe driving and accessible alternatives to driving."

Some are working on it. The American Society on Aging, located in San Francisco, for one, devoted much of its five-day, 2011 annual conference to transportation talk. Among topics covered: "Helping Non-Driving Seniors Use Community Transportation Options," "Supplemental Transportation Programs: What Will Work in Your Community?" and "Transportation and Socialization for Seniors." [94, 95, 96]

These and other presentations at the conference described how citizen groups, governments and private enterprise can join forces successfully to support older suburbanites who outlive their driving ability and risk losing touch with family and friends.

Noting that "in a car-oriented culture, access to an automobile is critical to mobility," other speakers looked ahead to a fusion of private automobiles and information technology coming to the rescue of an overworked, traditional mass transit system unable to keep up with the ballooning numbers of retired drivers.

At a preconference session, The National Center on Senior Transportation reviewed various "dementia-friendly" transportation resources and emerging "mobility-management" programs. The aim: To transfer transit agencies from their traditional role as operators of a fixed-route service to a novel part as single-stop, customized coordinators of a full range of transportation options to meet the needs of a specific community. [97]

As the topic of senior mobility becomes the talk of the town, the information superhighway and other outlets hum with news on new resources and revisions in existing ones. Thus, it's important for those on the go to keep in the know.

"It's all about having alternative ways to get to your desired destination, so be sure to use all available resources, not just the familiar ones," Gurwell advises.

"They may point you in directions you haven't thought of. An end to driving doesn't have to be depressing. There is light at the end of the tunnel."

16. When Dad Stopped Driving
by Jessie Thorpe

My mother's licensed driving career ended at age 87 with a crash a block from church. She collided with a friend, a member of her Sunday school class, who somehow didn't notice or heed the stop sign. Mother gave me her keys. She had asked me to tell her when it was time, but as it turned out I didn't have to. It wasn't her fault but she'd had enough. Unfortunately, not everyone is that wise.

– Gene K., 85

When my father turned 85 years old, his driver's license came up for renewal. I was visiting my parents at the time to help my mother through a course of chemotherapy for her colon cancer. It became immediately apparent this issue of the license had elevated the level of fuming in their household. At one point, Mother whispered to me that she hoped the State of Florida would solve what had become an imperative in her mind: Dad needed to stop driving.

This came as a shock to me. My father not driving? Impossible to imagine!

He was born in Detroit in 1903 at a time when automobiles were beginning to mix on the road with horse-drawn carriages and delivery wagons. Licensing did not exist, and before he had even reached his teens, he was driving trucks for his father's bedding and furniture business.

When Dad was 16, his father died suddenly of a burst appendix, and he and an older cousin took over the company. At that relatively young age, he left school to support his mother, not unusual in those days. Because he was blessed with a good mind, he became a lifelong "student" and made sure all four of his children –

my two sisters, our brother and me – graduated from college.

Apart from the difficulties, that life-altering event also gave Dad great independence and a healthy income. One of his indulgences was to own flashy cars during his drawn-out bachelor years. He used to regale us with stories of his Packards and sleek touring cars. He said that once he had the exact same car as the queen of the Netherlands – his model in bright green and orange.

How we ate that up! By the time he became a family man, however, at age 38, he was driving sedate sedans. They were always big, roomy cars. He liked Fords and Chryslers because they had large backseats and huge trunks. One black Mercury he drove had a red-leather front bench seat as wide and comfortable as a living-room sofa.

In those pre-seatbelt days you could pack in a lot of family for road trips. And did we travel! How Dad loved to be on the road. We went every summer up to the birch-tree-lined shores of Lake Huron. We frequently visited our grandparents in the hills of Pennsylvania slightly southeast of Pittsburgh. The harsh Michigan winters were an excuse for Dad to head south every February for a respite from snow and ice. He would drive Mom to Ft. Lauderdale, Florida, every year, and they stayed for a month. About every other year, even when we children were in school, they took us along. We were expected to keep up our studies, of course, but, oh, what freedom and what an escape!

Road trips are as much a part of my family memories as holidays. I think Dad was never happier than when he faced a ribbon of highway. He had begun his driving life when it could be quite a challenge, when paved roads were rare outside of cities. Gas stations and repair shops did not appear at regular intervals. He had to stay alert and know what he was doing.

Even in the 1950s and '60s, when we did so much family travel, the interstate system was only under construction. There might be a stretch of good four-lane highway for awhile, but then it would shrink back to two-lane blacktop, winding through little towns, where it was easy to get stuck in traffic clogs. Nowadays, people often want to get off the interstates and amble along scenic by-ways, but that can quickly become tedious, especially when you get stuck in a line behind a pokey tractor or must stop for a 100-car freight train on a hot day. I remember those train stops: the clanging and lowering striped bar, opening all the doors to get out of the un-air-conditioned car, standing on the blistering asphalt, counting the endless tankers and boxcars and then choking on exhaust when all the stopped cars started up at once.

Dad loved it. He never cared how long a trip was or how troublesome; he just liked being in his car, rolling along, figuring out his moves – "making time," as he called it. His quick temper was even in check most of the time, and when we children grew bored with our coloring books and playing the alphabet game or spotting license plates and started to fuss, he didn't say much more than, "Pipe down!"

He never flew on an airplane – not once. The story was he knew someone in his youth who was killed in a crash, and therefore Dad for his entire life considered flying unsafe. The road was his friend. He did get on large boats – once in particular when he took Mom to Europe, first class, on the famed S.S. France – and he was quite fond of train travel. But given any reasonable choice, he would slide under the wheel and take off for anywhere. One time he drove from Atlanta, Georgia, to Detroit in just one day – a feat he talked about proudly for years.

So I didn't know what to make of Mom's new (to me) anxiety about Dad's driving. He had always been a king of the road and proud of his perfect record – no tickets in over 70 years on the road. But Mom insisted things were different now.

Dad was "slipping."

My sisters and brother and I knew that our father was not exactly young anymore. But Mom was almost 15 years younger, and the two of them had always been so active and, well, youthful. We had kept in touch with them constantly, but at the time of Mom's anxiety about Dad's driving, we "girls" were in our early 40s and our "baby brother" was barely into his 30s. We were scattered on both coasts and in between, and maybe we didn't always see the reality of our parents' lives.

Mom's cancer had certainly focused our attention.

In those days I spent with them, Dad went over and over his strategy concerning the Department of Motor Vehicles. He had been to Kevin, his doctor, he said. Kevin, a chiropractor, had told him he was fine to drive, and if they gave him any guff about it to just call him. I wasn't sure how authoritative Kevin's opinion would be in the face of a failed eye exam or some such test, but Dad clung to this show of support.

I grew nervous about how this little drama would play out. Mother grew quiet; she had so many things to worry about.

I lay awake a couple of nights wondering what to do. Should I call my siblings and try to arrange some sort of phone intervention? I couldn't tell just how bad Dad's driving had gotten; while I was there, he did all his usual errands with no mishaps. What if this fixation of Mom's was a side effect of her illness and treatment? And how would they manage, if Dad stopped driving?

My only other experience with an elderly driver was my maternal grandfather. One day he was returning home from playing golf at his club and suddenly saw two center lines instead of one. He made it home, parked his white Buick in the garage and said he was done. After that, he had two of his grandsons who lived nearby chauffer him around. It seemed an elegant solution.

Yet in the case of my parents, all of us children lived so far away, and we could not be much help.

My thoughts churned. How would Mom get to her appointments? Public transportation hardly existed where they lived. Perhaps they could take cabs or hire a driver. All of this seemed abrupt and confusing. We had been dealing intensely with Mom's disease, and now this other trauma — and it would be a trauma if my Dad was grounded! My mother taking over the family driving responsibilities didn't seem like a workable solution at all.

Mom had always had her own car, beginning in her teen years, and we had all heard the story of her first little red roadster – to go

with her red hair. It was the tag end of the Depression, and her father said if she lived at home while going to college he'd buy her a
car. That was fine with Mom. Her older sisters and brother had gone
away to school, but Mom enrolled in Carnegie Tech (now Carnegie
Mellon) and just loved it. When she married Dad shortly after grad-
uation, even though it was wartime, she had her own wheels –
rarely the case with women in those days. The two-car family did
not become common until sometime in the '50s.

Mom used to drive us everywhere – even from Michigan back
to Pittsburgh to visit our grandparents. Later, when we became
teenagers, she allowed us to drive her cars. I remember particularly a two-toned red and white Ford, very cool, and a dark blue
Mercury with an unusual rear window that slanted inward and at
the touch of a button disappeared into the trunk.

We never drove Dad's cars. He said if any of us had an accident
in his car, someone could sue the company and take everything he
had. I never knew if that was true, but in any event his cars were off
limits.

Because of the age difference between them, Mom was only in
her late 40s when Dad retired. Rather rapidly they sold the house
in Detroit, keeping a cottage on a small lake near Ann Arbor, and
moved to Florida. We all visited frequently, and as the years passed
I noticed certain changes. For one thing, Mom no longer had her
own charge cards and checking account because Dad wanted to
"simplify" the finances. That seemed fairly normal, something
many retired couples did. But Dad also decided they needed only
one car. He had more time now, he said, and he could just drive
Mom wherever she needed to go.

The one-car thing didn't raise any alarms at first; it also seemed
like a normal retirement decision. It took a small but rather dra-
matic event for me to see how this change had affected Mom's life.

About seven or eight years into their retirement, Mom flew up
to Washington, D.C., to visit me and my family. From there I was
going to drive her and my two small daughters to Michigan for a
stay at the cottage on Winan's Lake. We stopped for lunch along

the Pennsylvania Turnpike, and as we were walking out to the car afterward, Mom asked me if she could drive for awhile. "Sure," I said, and I gave her a brief overview of the gear shift, turn signals and such in my Mercury Zephyr.

Then we took off, rolling along the merge lane into the always rushing traffic of the pike. She hadn't been driving even five minutes before I knew something was seriously wrong. Mom could not keep the car in a steady direction; she kept drifting toward the shoulder or across the lane line. Then I saw her head droop down in a drowsy way and told her to pull over. It was difficult for her even to judge her speed and slow down properly. We bounced and screeched to a stop.

"Mom," I said, "what's happening?"

She could not talk at that moment, but as we switched seats and I resumed the driving, she began to relate a shocking reality. She almost never drove anymore, she told me, and she had just wanted to try to "get back into it."

What?! My lovely vibrant mother, still with her natural flaming hair; a woman who got up every day and walked the neighborhood or swam in her pool, who played 18 holes of golf without tiring – this woman could no longer drive with confidence and skill? I decided I would try to remedy this, and during our days at the lake I had her drive around on the sparsely trafficked roads to regain her comfort behind the wheel. It really helped. She decided she would insist that Dad surrender the car keys from time to time and allow her to drive herself to the store or to visit friends.

In the years that followed, I was never sure how the plan was working. It always seemed as though Dad was still very much in charge in that area. Many times during our visits, he insisted he would drive us to the mall and then wait for us to do our shopping. It was awkward. We could never relax, knowing he was parked somewhere or sitting with his newspaper, clocking the minutes until we returned. I didn't know what to do. Mom became increasingly restricted. It was lucky she had many friends who would pick her up for luncheons, bridge games and such.

In fairness, I think Dad regarded it as a favor to her to do the driving. In his mind, he was helping. But in all my life, I never saw Mom in the driver's seat and Dad riding as her passenger. Not once. So now it seemed impossible that Dad would give up driving and Mom would become the chauffer.

Having absorbed all this, I became nervous as the day approached for Dad to renew his license. Mom wanted me to go with him, and I agreed; if anything happened, one of us should be there.

I had begun to observe Dad closely. For quite awhile, he had complained of pain in his knee, attributing it to bursitis – hence the chiropractor. He had started using a cane, even though his gait still appeared strong and purposeful. In the evenings, he would often rub Absorbine, Jr., an astringent, into his feet, saying they bothered him at times. At some point, around age 70, he had given up his beloved Stetsons, except for dress occasions, and wore softer shoes and thicker socks.

His hearing seemed to come and go. There were moments when he couldn't grasp what you were saying to him, but then if you whispered something in the next room he would shout, "I can hear that!"

These seemed like minor infirmities, but the problems with his eyes were not. I don't think Dad ever went for an official eye exam. He truly hated doctors and preferred to treat himself with vitamins and home remedies. I have lived to have proper doctors recommend sea weed or kelp tablets to me, which Dad had been ingesting decades earlier. As children, my siblings and I used to giggle about his potions – in particular a dreadful supposed cure-all mixture of vinegar and honey.

And yet, over the years, I have to say many of his ideas and habits have become the basis for the organic food culture and homeopathic medicines. He was an early believer – going back to the '30s – in vegetable juices, for instance. He would prepare awful concoctions for us of carrots, parsley and other bitter ingredients. As a young man, he fell in love with Florida in part because of the fresh juice bars located on practically every corner. In that regard, he was way ahead of his time.

We all knew Dad was physically healthy, but could his regular carrot juice drinks eliminate the need for prescription lenses? As he grew older, Dad would purchase stronger reading glasses from the drugstore and use those along with a huge, thick magnifying glass to read the stock tables in The Wall Street Journal.

This thing with the eyes could be a stumbling block to his license renewal. I was quite sure that Florida, just like every other state, asked applicants to read a chart before giving out a driver's license.

I could tell Dad was nervous the day we drove to the DMV. He was talking too loudly and blustering about other drivers on the road. His standard way of coping with fear was to get angry. As we walked in, he held onto my arm with his left hand and slammed his cane down hard with his right. When his number was called, we approached the window. I noticed his hand was trembling as he hung his cane on the counter and shoved papers at the woman official.

I thought perhaps she would take note of the cane, but she barely looked at him.

"Do you wear your glasses for driving?" she asked.

"Yes," said Dad. No mention was made about whether his glasses were prescribed for driving.

The official indicated the eye chart on a screen at her left and told him to read the fourth line.

"I can't see that," Dad barked.

"Well, what can you read?" she said.

Dad read the second line, three letters.

She didn't react in any way I could detect but simply stamped and shuffled the papers in front of her. In about a minute, she handed Dad an approval for his new license and sent him to the next line for a photo.

That was that; Dad was renewed for six years, to age 91.

He was ecstatic; I was shocked. I had hoped he would be placed under some sort of restriction – unable to drive at night, for instance. All this worry and drama turned out to be for nothing. No authority, it appeared, would make any sort of careful assessment of Dad's driving or limit him in any way.

Mom wasn't happy but could make no further protest. It was a done deal.

In the months that followed, as Mom's illness progressed, our family spent most of our time taking care of her and making sure she had every possible medical option. We all tried to keep her life as full and normal as we could. But we remained concerned about Dad's driving, especially when he began to have a few fender benders.

Still, these episodes took a back seat when compared to what was happening to Mom. We had so much to think about and do.

I was privileged, truly, to accompany my parents on their last road trip together, going from Florida to Michigan. It was May, and Mom wanted to be at her adored cottage and lake again. It took four days, me riding in back while they kibitzed and laughed, noting all the familiar landmarks of their many years making that drive. It was difficult, though, because Mom could not rest well or be comfortable, and I couldn't find the right foods for her on the road.

Rest stops were a challenge; they both needed help getting to the facilities. Nevertheless, that trip is a memory I cherish, even though Dad's driving unnerved me at times. I didn't think he moved his foot quickly enough to the brake at times. I was certain he could not see distances, and he regularly missed road signs. I stayed on high alert the entire trip.

After Mom passed away, later that summer, our attention refocused on Dad and his mobility.

Here was an 85-year-old man with diminishing physical abilities who, we decided, could no longer live alone so far from his family. His mind was practically as sharp as ever, but without his wife and lifelong partner, his world had shifted, and we knew he could not manage as well.

After many discussions, we persuaded him that the best solution would be for him to live with my family and "get his bearings."

The resulting upheaval was enormous. Looking back, I'm more

aware of what a huge and brave act it was for him to agree to move to Virginia within a month of Mom's death. My older sister and her husband rode with him to my house, with the few possessions he wanted to keep – mainly his car, a deep blue Crown Victoria, the car "all the cops drove." He arrived with few plans for the future except to continue driving.

Because my neighborhood was unfamiliar, I rode with him and navigated. Eventually, he managed to drive to our local strip mall to do small errands, but I stayed nervous whenever he was gone. We kept the Florida house intact for months, and he nurtured a secret dream of going back there to live – assisted by a fantasy housekeeper who would facilitate his life as before. It was hard for him to give up that conceit and agree the house should not stand empty and must be sold.

My siblings converged on Ft. Lauderdale to help dismantle the house – quite a project. After everything was sorted and packed and loaded onto a huge van or given to charity, my brother and younger sister and I were left with the task of getting Dad back to Virginia – in his car, naturally.

That last road trip is one we have never forgotten and never will. Dad insisted on driving. We decided not to argue and hoped we could take over at some point along the way. The first day, that did not happen. My brother rode shotgun, and my sister and I sat in the back, at times passing notes back and forth like schoolchildren.

What a harrowing trip! We were scared all the way up Interstate 95 with its relentless traffic. Even Dad was in a highly emotional state, having just seen his dream house emptied and his life stuffed into boxes. We were very aware of his mood, but we could not force him to give up his place behind the wheel. We were in our 30s and 40s, but we were still his children and somewhat intimidated by his authority over us. We loved and respected him greatly, and our devotion would not allow us to go against his decisions.

Worse, for two days going north, the weather grew colder, something Dad had always hated. His fear increased, and so did his anger, of course. His driving grew erratic: narrow misses when passing, drifts over the center line, missing a pull-off lane for a rest stop and pretending he had intended to go on to the next one. We just kept our eyes peeled and tried to intervene if he started to veer in the wrong direction. Not the greatest plan.

On the second day, we got as far as Fredericksburg, Virginia, and needed to stop for gas. My brother had told me Dad could no longer "feel the road" when he needed to slow down or change speeds. As we approached the gas pumps, Dad just kept rolling. My brother called out to him to stop, almost shouting, but Dad could not, and we came to a halt somewhere at the edge of the parking lot.

I jumped out and said I'd take Dad to the men's room and for my brother to pull the car over and gas up. When we returned, I calmly escorted Dad to the passenger side and got behind the wheel, telling him I was taking over the driving.

He was furious. He said he wanted to find a motel and stay the night on the road. I replied that we were only about an hour from home and we were going on. I won that fracas but not with much dignity. It didn't matter; by that time, our nerves were shot.

As the months passed, Dad kept on driving, and I continued to ride with him. My dear husband would not forbid me to do that, but he did say our two daughters could no longer go anywhere with Grandpa, and he was right. Sometimes Dad would let me drive him in his car, especially after one of his two-martini lunches.

He finally gave up the keys only when, one day, out of the blue and for no reason, he pulled into the parking lot of our townhouse community and side-swiped my car. He walked into the house and put his keys down on the table. That was it. It was over – not with a bang but a whimper, as T.S. Eliot wrote about the end of the world.

Well, let's not call it a whimper and not a defeat, either. Dad made his decision, one I think he'd been contemplating for a long time.

I felt nothing but relief. My siblings and I have often expressed our dismay that we could not – or, in any event, we did not – confront Dad. We were just grateful that he did not hurt himself or anyone else.

During his remaining year and a half, he did what he could to enjoy life. His head and heart (the "old ticker" he called it) stayed strong, but the zest had faded. His other children begged him to visit and offered to drive him, but he always declined. His days on the road had ended.

Yet, in one sense, they did not.

Widowed myself before 50, driving became a sort of combined therapy and pleasure for me. It also became an exercise in learning how to be alone. I drove out to Oklahoma to bury my husband in his hometown and then took a long, circuitous way back, stopping to visit friends along the way. With one daughter starting college and the other starting a career, I had time and the desire to travel. In the intervening years, I have driven to New England, out to Colorado and the Southwest, to the Dakotas and Montana and Wyoming. And many other places.

Almost always, during those times, I felt a sense of Dad riding along. What is this thing Edith Wharton called "the romance of the road?" I think it's a love of freedom, of being unencumbered somehow, of being lifted from care. When one is sailing along, alone with one's thoughts and the rhythm of pavement, the feeling is magnificent. The inside of a car can be a perfectly ordered, sane and contained world – for a time, anyway, a domain.

Sometimes, returning from a trip when the day has grown late, I begin calculating minutes and miles and ask myself whether I should stop or try to make it to the comfort of my bed. That's when I think of Dad and his famous run from Atlanta to Detroit, of his peak years of calm and control in his perfect realm. I'll murmur, "Okay, Dad, bring me home."

He has, every time.

I don't know if there is a driving gene, but if there is, I have it. Now at an age where I'm aware that I need to re-focus on my driving, I'm grateful for whatever props can help me stay on the road, particularly my prescription glasses. I know I need to be more cautious, mind speed limits and watch out at turns. Driving my grandchildren around keeps me sharp and aware that I'm transporting precious cargo. Above all, I do not want to give this up. I love it too much.

I adore driving along country roads and savoring what remains of rural America. I love the independence of getting into my car and going exactly where I want to go, taking whatever time I need. I have taught myself to be a good and patient passenger when that is called for, but my preference is to be in the command position. That's the truth.

One night while driving home from my daughter's house, the sky was glowing a rosy gold, and I didn't quite want the day to end. It occurred to me that I could just keep driving – all the way to California, if I wished. My car was in good shape; I had my credit cards and everything I needed for a road trip. The idea raced around my brain and filled me with an incredible strength of possibility.

Being out in the open, with a long road ahead snaking into an unclear future, some unseen hand building what appears to be a vision of cloud heaven on the horizon, is pure joy. I can sing; I can talk to whomever I wish in my imagination; I can think outrageous things, even that I am young again.

If I could, I'd do it forever.

About the Authors

Phil Berardelli is a journalist with over 40 years of experience. He has covered such topics as energy, science, education and popular culture as well as highway safety. His work has appeared in The Washington Post, Washington Times, Los Angeles Times, Pittsburgh Post-Gazette and many other newspapers and magazines. He has been an editor with McGraw-Hill, Time-Life and United Press International. His background also includes several years as a middle-school teacher and six years as producer and co-host of a weekly television program, "The Moviegoing Family," which appeared in the Washington, D.C., area and nationally on The Learning Channel. Born in Pittsburgh, Pennsylvania, he has lived in Northern Virginia since 1970 and western Maryland since 2008.

Dr. Robert A. Comunale is a semi-retired physician in family practice and a specialist in aviation medicine who lives and works out of his home office in McLean, Virginia. He has published three novels and two short-story collections, all based on the character of his alter ego, Dr. Robert Galen. He also enjoys gardening, electronics, pounding on a piano, and yelling at his dimwitted cat. He describes himself as an eccentric and iconoclast. The cat has provided no comment.

John Matras is an award-winning auto writer who filed his first article in Custom Rodder magazine in 1980. Since then he has written for all of the big car magazines – Car and Driver, Road & Track, Motor Trend, AutoWeek, Automobile – plus a variety of others. He is founder and editor-in-chief of CarBuzzard.com, an eclectic site full of car reviews, news and, as he puts it, "stuff found on the side of the road." John has also written four automotive books: a history of the Mazda RX-7 and buyers' guides for Mazda, Datsun/Nissan and Volvo. And with Matt Stone, former editor of Motor Trend, he co-authored 365 Cars You Must Drive. John has three adult daughters, two son-in-laws and one grandson, and he has been married for more than four wonderful decades to Mary Ann Matras, Distinguished Professor of Mathematics at East Stroudsburg University of Pennsylvania.

Lidia Wasowicz Pringle is an author and free-lance writer who spent 30 years with United Press International. She has written more than 3,000 articles that have appeared in publications around the world, including Paris Match, the Hong Kong Standard, Pacific Stars and Stripes, Times of India, The New York Times, The Washington Post and Los Angeles Times. She has been twice nominated for the Pulitzer Prize, and her professional awards include Outstanding Journalist of California Award, five UPI Outstanding Coverage Awards, first-place writing awards from a variety of press clubs and journalism organizations, and the Lincoln Steffens Journalism Award for investigative reporting. She lives in Tiburon, California, with her husband, daughter and a Samoyed named Taffy.

Jessie Thorpe is Acquisitions Editor for Mountain Lake Press. For 10 years previously she worked as a freelance writer and copy editor, providing research and editorial support for international business concerns. The author of two novels, she also worked as a book critic and essayist for United Press International. Born in Detroit, Michigan, she has lived in Northern Virginia since 1968 and western Maryland since 2008.

Dr. Allan F. Williams is a social psychologist with a Ph.D. from Harvard University. He was employed for more than 30 years by the Insurance Institute for Highway Safety, retiring as Chief Scientist in 2004. Since that time he has consulting and lectured on highway safety issues. He is the author of more than 350 articles on a variety of highway safety topics, including many dealing with age-related factors in crash involvement. He lives in Bethesda, Maryland.

Notes

1   "Car plows through market, killing 9," CNN.com, July 17, 2003.

2. "Woman drives car into Sears," Orlando Sentinel, October 10, 2006.

3. Schwartz, Terry and Bishop, Stewart, "Mother and baby injured as car crashes into Danvers Wal-Mart," Boston.com, June 2, 2009.

4. Arnold, Keba, "Woman, 73, was driving husband to Vietnam Memorial," Crashesinto.com, June 3, 2009.

5. Li, Guohua; Braver, Elisa R. and Chen, Li-Hui, "Fragility versus excessive crash involvement as determinants of high death rates per vehicle-mile of travel among older drivers," Accident Analysis and Prevention, 35 (2003) 227–235.

6. Cheung, Ivan and McCartt, Anne T., "Declines in Fatal Crashes of Older Drivers: Changes in Crash Risk and Survivability," Insurance Institute for Highway Safety, June 2010.

7   Braitman, Keli A.; Chaudhary, Neil K. and McCartt, Anne T., "Effect of Passenger Presence on Older Drivers' Risk of Fatal Crash Involvement," Insurance Institute for Highway Safety, March 2011.

8   Stalvey, Beth T. and Owsley, Cynthia, "Self-perceptions and Current Practices of High-risk Older Drivers: Implications for Driver Safety Interventions," Journal of Health Psychology, July 2000, Vo. 5, No. 4, pp. 441-456.

9   Physician's Guide to Assessing and Counseling Older Drivers, 2nd edition, American Medical Association, February 3, 2010.

10 Grabowski, David C.; Campbell, Christine M. and Morrisey, Michael A., "Elderly Licensure Laws and Motor Vehicle Fatalities," Journal of the American Medical Association, 2004; 291(23), pp. 2840-2846.

11 Ageing and Transportation: Mobility Needs and Safety Issues, Organisation for Economic Co-Operation and Development, 2001.

12 Carr, David B.; Schwartzberg, Joanne G.; Manning, Lela, and

Sempek, Jessica, "Physician's Guide to Assessing and Counseling Older Drivers, 2nd edition," Washington, D.C., NHTSA, 2010, p. 3.

Pellerito, Joseph M., "The Effects of Driving Retirement on Elderly Men and Women Living in Metropolitan Detroit," Topics in Geriatric Rehabilitation, April/June 2009, Volume 25, Issue 2, p 135-153; DOI: 10.1097/TGR.ob013e3181a1038d.

Pellerito, Joseph M., "Driving Retirement and the Quality of Life of Older Men and Women Living in Metropolitan Detroit," ETD Collection for Wayne State University, Paper AAI3320211, January 1, 2008.

Pellerito, Joseph M., "The Effects of Driving Retirement on Elderly Men and Women Living in Metropolitan Detroit."

13 Ibid.

14 AARP, "Why Take a Driver Safety Class?"

15 AAA Foundation for Traffic Safety, "Drive Safe, Drive Sharp."

16 National Highway Traffic Safety Administration, "Older Driver Program, Five-Year Strategic Plan," 2012-2017, p. 1.

17 "Defensive Driving" and "Driver Seat Game," two examples from a host of available programs.

18 Carr, David B.; Schwartzberg, Joanne G.; Manning, Lela, and Sempek, Jessica, "Physician's Guide to Assessing and Counseling Older Drivers, 2nd edition," p. 2.

19 Ibid., p. 1-19.

California Department of Motor Vehicles, "Senior Guide for Safe Driving," 2007, p. 1-13.

National Highway Traffic Safety Administration, "Safe Driving for Older Adults."

California Department of Motor Vehicles, "Senior Driver."

American Medical Association, "Why Are Older Drivers at Risk?"

20. Carr, David B.; Schwartzberg, Joanne G.; Manning, Lela, and Sempek, Jessica, "Physician's Guide to Assessing and Counseling Older Drivers, 2nd edition, p. 145-187.

California Department of Motor Vehicles, "Senior Guide...," p. 13.

21 California Department of Motor Vehicles, "Senior Guide...," p. 2-5.

American Medical Association, "Why Are Older Drivers at Risk?"

22 Milloy, Courtland, "Centenarian's advice won't steer you wrong," The Washington Post, August 12, 2012.

23 Carr, David B.; Schwartzberg, Joanne G.; Manning, Lela, and Sempek, Jessica, "Physician's Guide...," p. 12.

24 Ibid.

25 Ibid., p. 11.

26 California Department of Motor Vehicles, "Senior Driver," "Vision Tests."

American Medical Association, "Why Are Older Drivers at Risk?"

27 National Highway Traffic Safety Administration, "Safe Driving for Older Adults."

28 Ibid.

29 Carr, David B.; Schwartzberg, Joanne G.; Manning, Lela, and Sempek, Jessica, "Physician's Guide...," p. 3.

30 Ibid.

31 Ibid.

32 American Medical Association, "Why Are Older Drivers at Risk?"

California Department of Motor Vehicles, "Senior Driver."

33 Kirk I. Erickson, Michelle W. Voss, Ruchika Shaurya Prakash, Chandramallika Basak, Amanda Szabo, Laura Chaddock, Jennifer S. Kim, Susie Heo, Heloisa Alves, Siobhan M. White, Thomas R. Wojcicki, Emily Mailey, Victoria J. Vieira, Stephen A. Martin, Brandt D. Pence, Jeffrey A. Woods, Edward McAuley, and Arthur F. Kramerb, "Exercise training increases size of hippocampus and improves memory," Proceedings of the National Academy of Sciences, February 15, 2011, Vol. 108 No. 7, pp. 3017-3022.

34 American Medical Association, "Why Are Older Drivers at Risk?"

California Department of Motor Vehicles, "Senior Driver."

35 National Institute of Neurological Disorders and Stroke, "Dementia: Hope Through Research."

36 American Medical Association, "Why Are Older Drivers at Risk?"

California Department of Motor Vehicles, "Senior Driver."

Carr, David B.; Schwartzberg, Joanne G.; Manning, Lela, and Sempek, Jessica, "Physician's Guide...," p.157.

37   Reger, Mark A.; Welsh, Robert K.; Watson, G. Stennis; Cholerton, Brenna; Baker, Laura D., and Craft, Suzanne, "The Relationship Between Neuropsychological Functioning and Driving Ability in Dementia: A Meta-Analysis," Neuropsychology, 2004, Vol. 18, No. 1, p. 85–93; DOI: 10.1037/0894-4105.18.1.85.

38   California Department of Motor Vehicles, "Senior Driver."

39   Reger, Mark A.; Welsh, Robert K.; Watson, G. Stennis; Cholerton, Brenna; Baker, Laura D., and Craft, Suzanne, "The Relationship..."

40   Betts, Lisa R.; Taylor, Christopher P.; Sekuler, Allison B., and Bennett, Patrick J., "Aging Reduces Center-Surround Antagonism in Visual Motion Processing," Neuron, February 3, 2005, Vol. 45, No. 3, p. 361-366.

Tadin, Duje, and Blake, Randolph, "Motion Perception Getting Better with Age?" Neuron, February

3, 2005, Vol. 45, No. 3, p. 325-327.

Tadin, Duje; Lappin, Joseph S., and Blake, Randolph, "Fine Temporal Properties of Center–Surround Interactions in Motion Revealed by Reverse Correlation," The Journal of Neuroscience, March 8, 2006, Vol. 26, No.10, p. 2614-2622; doi:10.1523/JNEUROSCI.4253-05.2006.

Tadin, Duje, et al, "Improved Motion Perception and Impaired Spatial Suppression following Disruption of Cortical Area MT/V5," The Journal of Neuroscience, January 26, 2011, Vol. 31, No. 4, p.1279-1283.

Glasser, Davis M.; Tsui, James M.G.; Pack, Christopher C., and Tadin, Duje, "Perceptual and Neural Consequences of Rapid Motion Adaptation," Proceedings of the National Academy of Sciences, June 28, 2011, Vol. 108, No. 26, published ahead of print June 27, 2011; DOI:10.1073/pnas. 1101141108.

41   Ibid.

42   Tadin, Duje, et al, "Improved Motion Perception..."

43   Michael A. Yassa, Aaron T. Mattfeld, Shauna M. Stark and Craig E.L. Stark, "Age-related memory deficits linked to circuit-specific disruptions in the hippocampus," Proceedings of the National Academy of Sciences, May 9, 2011.

44   Yassa, Michael A.; Mattfeld, Aaron T.; Stark, Shauna M., and Stark, Craig E.L., "Age-Related Memory Deficits Linked to Circuit-Specific Disruptions in the Hippocampus," Proceedings of the National Academy of Sciences, May 10, 2011, Vol. 108, No. 29, published online before print,

May 9, 2011; DOI: 10.1073/pnas.1101567108.

45 Erickson, Kirk I.; Voss, Michelle W.; Prakash, Ruchika Shaurya; Basak, Chandramallika; Szabo, Amanda; Chaddock, Laura; Kim, Jennifer S.; Heo, Susie; Alves, Heloisa; White, Siobhan M.; Wojcicki, Thomas R.; Mailey, Emily; Vieira, Victoria J.; Martin, Stephen A.; Pence, Brandt D.; Woods, Jeffrey A.; McAuley, Edward, and Kramer, Arthur F., "Exercise Training Increases Size of Hippocampus and Improves Memory," Proceedings of the National Academy of Sciences, published online before print January 31, 2011, DOI: 10.1073/pnas.1015950108 PNAS.

46 David B.; Schwartzberg, Joanne G.; Manning, Lela, and Sempek, Jessica, "Physician's Guide...," p. 4.

47 California Department of Motor Vehicles, "Senior Guide...," p. 5.

48 Ibid., p. 6.

49 Ball, Karlene; Edwards, Jerri D.; Ross, Lesley A., and McGwin, Jr., Gerald, "Cognitive Training Decreases Motor Vehicle Collision Involvement of Older Drivers," Journal of the American Geriatrics Society, November 2010, Vol. 58, Issue 11, p. 2107-2113; first published online November 4, 2010, DOI: 10.1111/j.1532-5415.2010.03138.x.

50 Iverson, D.J.; Gronseth, G.S.; Reger, M.A.; Classen, S.; Dubinsky, R.M.; Rizzo, M., and Quality Standards Subcommittee of the American Academy of Neurology, "Practice Parameter Update: Evaluation and Management of Driving Risk in Dementia: Report of the Quality Standards Subcommittee of the American Academy of Neurology," Neurology, April 20, 2010, Vol. 74, No. 16, p. 1316-1324.

O'Neill, D., "Practice Parameter Update: Evaluation and Management of Driving Risk in Dementia: Report of the Quality Standards Subcommittee of the American Academy of Neurology," author reply, Neurology, November 2, 2010, Vol. 75, No. 18, p. 1659-1660.

51 Carr, David B.; Schwartzberg, Joanne G.; Manning, Lela, and Sempek, Jessica, "Physician's Guide...," p. 11.

52 Public Health Law Research, "Vision Screening for Older Drivers."

53 Iverson, D.J.; Gronseth, G.S.; Reger, M.A.; Classen, S.; Dubinsky, R.M.; Rizzo, M., and Quality Standards Subcommittee of the American Academy of Neurology, "Practice Parameter Update..."

54 Carr, David B.; Schwartzberg, Joanne G.; Manning, Lela, and Sempek, Jessica, "Physician's Guide...," p. 157.

55 Iverson, D.J.; Gronseth, G.S.; Reger, M.A.; Classen, S.; Dubinsky,

R.M.; Rizzo, M., and Quality Standards Subcommittee of the American Academy of Neurology, "Practice Parameter Update..."

56   Ibid.

57   Park, Alice, "Kids Are Safer in the Car With Their Grandparents Behind the Wheel," TIME Healthland, July 18, 2011.

58   Billera, Michael, "Florida Crashes: 11th Victim Found in I-75 Pileup," February 1, 2012.

59   National Highway Traffic Safety Administration, "Identifying Behaviors and Situations Associated With Increased Crash Risks for Older Drivers," June 2009, DOT HS 811 093, p. vii and p. 22.

60   U.S. Department of Transportation Federal Highway Administration, The National Intersection Safety Problem, FHWA SA 10-005, November 2009.

61   Kirk I. Erickson, Michelle W. Voss, Ruchika Shaurya Prakash, Chandramallika Basak, Amanda Szabo, Laura Chaddock, Jennifer S. Kim, Susie Heo, Heloisa Alves, Siobhan M. White, Thomas R. Wojcicki, Emily Mailey, Victoria J. Vieira, Stephen A. Martin, Brandt D. Pence, Jeffrey A. Woods, Edward McAuley, and Arthur F. Kramerb, "Exercise training increases size of hippocampus and improves memory," Proceedings of the National Academy of Sciences, February 15, 2011, Vol. 108 No. 7, pp. 3017-3022.

62   National Institute on Aging, "Is It Time to Give Up Driving?"

63   Flaherty, Mary Pat, "Elderly Couple Found Frozen to Death after Getting Lost During Drive," The Washington Post, January 13, 2011.

64   Insurance Institute for Highway Safety, "Q&A: Older Drivers," December 2010.

65   Insurance.com, "Baby Boomer Drivers Will Increase the Number of Senior Drivers," May 5, 2008.

66   Carr, David B.; Schwartzberg, Joanne G.; Manning, Lela, and Sempek, Jessica, "Physician's Guide...," p. 2.

67   Ibid.

68   Insurance Institute for Highway Safety, "Q&A: Older Drivers"

69   Ibid.

70   Carr, David B.; Schwartzberg, Joanne G.; Manning, Lela, and Sempek, Jessica, "Physician's Guide...," p. 5.

71 Ibid.

American Medical Association, "Older Driver Safety."

American Medical Association, "Why Are Older Drivers at Risk?"

72 Carr, David B.; Schwartzberg, Joanne G.; Manning, Lela, and Sempek, Jessica, "Physician's Guide...," p. 5.

73 Ibid., p. 52-53.

National Highway Traffic Safety Administration, "Talking with Older Drivers about Safe Driving."

74 Carr, David B.; Schwartzberg, Joanne G.; Manning, Lela, and Sempek, Jessica, "Physician's Guide...," p. 52-53.

75 Stephens, Burton W.; McCarthy, Dennis P.; Marsiske, Michael; Shechtman, Orit; Classen, Sherrilene; Justiss, Michael, and Mann, William C., "International Older Driver Consensus Conference on Assessment, Remediation and Counseling for Transportation Alternatives: Summary and Recommendations," Physical & Occupational Therapy in Geriatrics, November 2005, Vol. 23, No. 2-3, p. 103–121; DOI: 10.1300/J148v23n02_07.

California Department of Motor Vehicles, "Senior Guide...," p. 43.

Carr, David B.; Schwartzberg, Joanne G.; Manning, Lela, and Sempek, Jessica, "Physician's Guide...," p.50.

76 Carr, David B.; Schwartzberg, Joanne G.; Manning, Lela, and Sempek, Jessica, "Physician's Guide...," p. 13.

77 California Department of Motor Vehicles, "Senior Safe Mobility ... Driving Safer, Longer," p. 9

78 Ibid.

79 National Highway Traffic Safety Administration, "How to Understand and Influence Older Drivers," p. 1-12.

80 Ibid.

81 Carr, David B.; Schwartzberg, Joanne G.; Manning, Lela, and Sempek, Jessica, "Physician's Guide...," p. 4.

82 Ibid.

83 Ibid., p. 49.

84 Ibid.

85 Keenan, Teresa A., "Home and Community Preferences of the 45+ Population," 2010, AARP Research and Strategic Analysis, Washington, D.C., p. 2.

86 Ong, Anthony D., "Pathways Linking Positive Emotion and Health in Later Life," Current Directions in Psychological Science, December 2010, Vol. 19, No. 6, p. 358-362; DOI: 10.

87 Carr, David B.; Schwartzberg, Joanne G.; Manning, Lela, and Sempek, Jessica, "Physician's Guide...," p.54.

88 Ibid., p. 50.
The Hartford Insurance, "Older Driver Safety Conversations."

89 Carr, David B.; Schwartzberg, Joanne G.; Manning, Lela, and Sempek, Jessica, "Physician's Guide...," p.51.

90 Ibid.

91 Carr, David B.; Schwartzberg, Joanne G.; Manning, Lela, and Sempek, Jessica, "Physician's Guide...," p.51.

92 Ibid., p.55.

93 CNN.com, "Car plows through market, killing 9," July 17, 2003.

94 American Society on Aging, Aging in America, the 2011 Annual Conference of the American Society on Aging, April 26-30, 2011, San Francisco; Smith, Alice E., and Smith, Warren K., "Housing, Accessibility and Technology: Helping Non-Driving Seniors Use Community Transportation Options," April 27, 2011.

95 American Society on Aging, Aging in America, the 2011 Annual Conference of the American Society on Aging, April 26-30, 2011, San Francisco; Eberhard, John W.; Freund, Katherine; Huston, Barbara; Kerschner, Helen; Smith, Richard, and Wilcke, Julie, "Supplemental Transportation Programs: What Will Work in Your Community?" April 27, 2011.

96 American Society on Aging, Aging in America, the 2011 Annual Conference of the American Society on Aging, April 26-30, 2011, San Francisco; Burr, Betty; Goodrich, Corinne; Maltz, Jeff; Steiner, Susan, and Steiner, Saal, "Transportation and Socialization for Seniors," April 28, 2011.

97 American Public Transportation Association, "Mobility Management: A New Role for Public Transportation."